Charles Napier Bell

The Selkirk Settlement and the Settlers

A concise History of the Red River Country

Charles Napier Bell

The Selkirk Settlement and the Settlers
A concise History of the Red River Country

ISBN/EAN: 9783337151102

Printed in Europe, USA, Canada, Australia, Japan

Cover: Foto ©ninafisch / pixelio.de

More available books at **www.hansebooks.com**

"The Selkirk Settlement and the Settlers."

By CHARLES N. BELL, F.R.G.S.

HISTORY OF FUR TRADE.

About 1736 LaVerandyre, a French-Canadian, established on the Red river a trading post, which was certainly the first occasion that white men had a fixed abode in the lower Red River valley. After 1770 the English merchants and traders of Montreal sent fur traders, with assortments of goods, into the country west of Lake Superior, but it was not until the year 1796 that they, with the Hudson's Bay Co., established permanent posts on the Red and Assiniboine rivers. It is not clear, from the available records, why the trade of these districts was neglected, but it was presumably because the North Saskatchewan and Athabasca rivers afforded a sufficiently extensive field for the force of adventurers engaged in the fur trade. Certainly from the year 1796, both the Hudson's Bay Co. and the Northwest Co. had several regularly supplied posts on the Red and Assiniboine rivers, though some of them were abandoned from time to time, and rebuilt in the immediate neighborhood, as was the case at Pembina and the mouth of the Souris. For instance, at Pembina in 1796 Peter Grant erected a fort on the east bank of the Red river directly opposite the mouth of the Pembina river. In 1798 the post was on the south bank of the Pembina at its confluence with the Red and was under the charge of Charles Chabollier. Again in 1801 Alexander Henry built a fort on the north side of the Pembina, a few hundred yards from the deserted post on the south side. These were all forts of the Northwest Co.

On Sept. 28th, 1803, Alexander Henry left an assortment of trading goods with another officer of the Northwest Company at the Forks, which place was situated at the point between the Red River and the Assiniboine, on the north side of the latter. The next spring a large return of fur was shipped from this post to Fort William, on Lake Superior. It was not until 1806 that a fort of any considerable size was erected at the Forks, when at that date the Northwest Company built Fort Gibraltar, which was in after years the centre of very great interest to the Selkirk settlers.

The Hudson's Bay Company claim that they had a trading post on the Red River as early as 1796, and there is every reason to conclude that such a fort was in existence at a very early date in the history of the Red River settlement, and stood at the north end of the Slough at what is now known as East Selkirk village. Mr. Donald Murray, one of the Selkirk colonists, informs me that he slept at the ruins of such a place in the fall of 1815, when arriving in this country. He states that it was an old post of the Hudson's Bay Company, and had been called Ft. William. The chimneys still stood, in a ruined condition, in 1815. Both the rival fur companies also had trading posts at Netley Creek, below Selkirk, on the west side of the Red River.

A third fur company, called the X Y Company, numbering amongst its partners Sir Alexander Mackenzie and Edward Ellice, competed in the fur trade on the Red and Assiniboine rivers, between 1800 (perhaps a year or two before) and 1804, when an amalgamation took place between it and the Northwest Co.

In 1804 a large number of "freemen," or discharged employees of the different fur companies, found their way to the vicinity of the trading-posts on the Red and Assiniboine rivers, a small settlement also being made by them on the Pembina river, at the place where it issues from the Pembina mountains, then called the Hair Hills. These freemen were nearly all of French extraction, being either Canadas or the issue of French-Canadian fathers and Indian women. It has been claimed that the first white woman who arrived in the Red River country was a French-Canadian, Madame Lajimoniere, who came to the Northwest from Three Rivers, Quebec, in 1806. I have found in the unpublished journal of Alexander Henry, an officer of the Northwest Company, a record of the fact that in 1807 an Orkney girl, disguised as a boy, who had followed her lover out from the Orkney Islands, gave birth to a child at Pembina. But Henry speaks of the wives of some of the Northwest Company's officers residing at the posts on the Red river from 1800 to 1806 in such terms that it implies that they were not of Indian blood, so that investigation may yet show that white women were here prior to the above-mentioned two.

After the establishment of Fort Gibraltar in 1806, it would appear, from the slight amount of data available, that quite a number of French-Canadians and Metis settled on the Red river and erected dwellings, where their families resided during the winters and when the men were absent in the service of the Northwest Company. I can find nothing regarding the operations of the Hudson's Bay Company for some years after 1808, but it is likely that they continued to trade on the two rivers as they, like the Northwest company, had posts on both streams when the Selkirk colonists arrived in 1812.

This leads us up to the date when matters in England were shaping themselves tending to the formation of a colony on the banks of the far-distant Red river, which afterwards resulted in a vast amount of trouble and considerable bloodshed before the colonists were allowed to settle down quietly to agricultural pursuits and in permanent abodes.

became anxious that their faces should be turned to some colony of the empire. On May 24th, 1799, on the death of his father, he succeeded to the earldom of Selkirk, his six brothers having died before that date, the last in 1797, when he took the title of Lord Daer and Shortcleugh.

From the time Selkirk visited the Highlands to 1802 he was striving to carry out some scheme which would bring relief to the peasantry there. After much correspondence with the British government regarding the colonizing of a large tract of land in the island of St. John, since named Prince Edward Island, he succeeded in a practical manner in carrying out his project. In August, 1803, 800 selected emigrants were landed at the colony, where, though meeting with very many

LORD SELKIRK.

Thomas Douglas, fifth Earl of Selkirk, Baron Daer and Shortcleugh in the Scotch peerage (1771-1820), was the seventh and youngest son of Dunbar (Hamilton) Douglas, the fourth earl. Born at the family seat in Kirkcudbrightshire, on the 20th June, 1771, he was educated at Edinburgh university, associating there with Sir Walter Scott, who in future years was a firm and steadfast friend.

As early as 1792 Selkirk interested himself in the state of the Highland peasantry, who were frequently evicted from their homes and forced to emigrate. He found, during a lengthened journey amongst these people, that the country was fast becoming pastoral, and the conviction was forced upon him, that emigration was the only hope left to the Highlanders, and with the true instincts of a British subject, he

difficulties, they eventually succeeded beyond their most sanguine expectations, their descendants to-day numbering many thousands of the population of the island.

Lord Selkirk, after personally superintending the placing of the colony, (which he revisited the following year) undertook an extended tour through the United States and Canada. Letters are on fyle in the Archives Department at Ottawa which show that he was endeavoring to establish settlements in Upper Canada as far west as the Sault St. Marie. In 1803 he proposed to the Government of Upper Canada to construct a wagon road from his colony of Baldoon, in Kent county, to Toronto, at a cost of over £40,000, if the government would give him a grant of certain crown lands at points along the road; but the government would not agree with him as to valuation of the lands, and the project fell through. Selkirk wrote a number of works on "The necessity of a more effective system of national defence," "Parliamentary Reform," etc. The first-named ran through two, and the last through three editions.

SELKIRK TURNS HIS ATTENTION TO THE RED RIVER.

During Selkirk's visit to Montreal he had been received and entertained by the resident partners of the Northwest Fur Co., who took every opportunity of paying him attention. They afforded him a very full insight into the management of their fur trade. It was written in 1817, by Edward Ellice (who, then a partner of the Northwest Co., afterwards became a director of the Hudson's Bay Co.) that Selkirk's enquiries were more extended than was usual in the case of foreign visitors, but that they little expected that their confidential communications to a person expressing his admiration at the result of their exertions, and his sincere friendship and thankful acknowledgments to themselves, should have awakened the spirit of self-interest, which subsequently became so apparent, and still less did they suppose they were placing means in the hands of a commercial rival, to be applied first in opposition to their trade, and after the failure of that experiment in an attempt to effect the ruin of their establishment.

Lord Selkirk went to England and began to arrange for the carrying out of a grand project which would give him a control of the management of the Hudson's Bay Company. Ellice states that Selkirk communicated his ideas to a gentleman "long interested in the Northwest Company, and to whom the public are indebted for a description of the country and of his own voyage and discoveries." This was most probably Sir Alexander Mackenzie, the discoverer of the Mackenzie River. This gentleman went into the scheme without any definite object further than a re-sale of the acquired stock at an enhanced price, when their management of the company's affairs had resulted favorably. Owing to bad management the stock of the Hudson's Bay Co. had fallen from 250 per cent to between 50 and 60; and no dividend had been paid for years. Large blocks of stock were purchased, but owing to disagreement the two associates parted and Selkirk retained the bulk at least of the acquired stock, if he did not hold it all. Lord Selkirk immediately obtained opinions from some of the highest legal authorities in England as to the powers possessed by the Hudson's Bay Co. under their charter of 1670. A full statement of these opinions is contained in the reports on the Ontario boundary question to the Canadian House of Commons in 1880. In a book

written and published by John Halkett, a relative of Selkirk, is given a very different version of this decision by these same legal authorities, and much more favorable to the Hudson's Bay Co. The former seems to be the most authentic. These opinions held that the company could exclude all persons from residing on the lands granted to them, and not already settled there. But they were of opinion that the company could not dispossess the Canadians of the posts already occupied by them when they had been 20 years in quiet possession. They could not prevent people from using the navigation of Hudson's Bay or the navigable rivers, or where they have been accustomed to pass for the purpose of transporting themselves and their merchandise, nor to prevent travellers from using wood and water, or pitching their tents. The company could not maintain a right to an exclusive trade. They had certain powers to act in administering justice.

These opinions were given by Samuel Romilly, G. S. Holroyd, W. M. Cruise, J. Scarlett and John Bell, but on the other hand the persons interested in the Northwest Company received opinions more favorable to them from equally eminent authorities.

Having extended his purchases of Hudson's Bay Company stock to the amount of nearly £40,000 (the whole amount at that time being about £100,000) he at once asserted his controlling influence and replaced several members of the committee by his relatives and friends. The general conduction of the affairs of the company immediately improved, but it was not for some time apparent what was the final object of his lordship. In May, 1811, a general meeting of the shareholders was called and those in attendance were informed that the Governor and committee considered it beneficial to their general interests to grant to Lord Selkirk, in fee simple, about 116,-000 square miles of territory in the Red River valley, on condition that he should establish a colony on the grant, and furnish, on certain terms, from among the settlers, such laborers as were required by the company in their trade. Several shareholders present (it is asserted by Ellice that all of them) protested against this grant to Selkirk, though it is significant that not less than two of the dissentients were men who were avowed agents of the Northwest Company, and Mr. Halkett writes that two of these persons had purchased their stock only forty-eight hours before the meeting, their object being to embarass the Hudson's Bay Company so that the Northwest Company would gain an advantage.

The boundaries of the district granted to Lork Selkirk under these circumstances were as follows:

"Beginning at the western shores of Lake Winnipeg at a point on 52° 50' north latitude, and thence running west to Lake

Winnipegoosis, otherwise called Little Winnipeg; thence into a southerly direction through said lake, so as to strike its western shore in latitude 52°; thence due west to the place where the parallel 52° intersects the western branch of the Red river, otherwise called the Assiniboine river; thence due south from that point of intersection to the heights of land which separate the waters running into the Hudson's Bay from those of the Missouri and Mississippi rivers; thence in an easterly direction along the height of land to the sources of the River Winnipeg, meaning by such last-named river the principal branch of the waters which unite in the Lake Saginagas; thence along the main stream of those waters, and the middle of the several lakes through which they flow, to the mouth of the River Winnipeg, and thence in a northerly direction through the middle of Lake Winnipeg to the place of beginning, which territory is called Assiniboia."

Certainly this was an extensive and valuable free gift, which cost the company, twenty-five years later, some £25,000 to regain possession of. It must, however, be borne in mind that an enormous outlay of money was necessary before the land would be of any direct value, though the idea appears to have been entertained by Lord Selkirk that he could sell the lands in England for a lump sum. This is indicated in the terms of the prospectus which he prepared, and to some extent circulated, though the assertion has been made that it was not intended for general circulation, but was composed only for the edification and information of some friends.

The shareholders who were opposed to the grant, in their protest took strong exception in detail, on the following general grounds: There was no adequate consideration stipulated for between the company and the earl. The land granted comprised 70,000 superficial miles, containing about 44,000,000 acres of the most valuable arable land, and constituted no inconsiderable portion of the company's capital stock. That if it was necessary to sell the land it should have been advertised. That the Earl was not sufficiently bound to settle the grant and that it would be difficult to people "a region 2,000 miles from any seaport, and out of reach of all those aids and comforts which are derived from civil society." That no reason could be seen for the grant but the endowing of Lord Selkirk's posterity with an immensely valuable landed estate. That private traffic would ensue between the Indians and the settlers, to the injury of the company's interests, and the settlement would become an asylum for deserters from the traders.

This protest was signed on the 30th May, 1811, by Wm. Thwaits, Robert Whitehead, John Inglis, John Fish, Edward Ellice and Alex. Mackenzie, but nothing resulted from it, and Lord Selkirk proceeded to carry out

his long cherished and difficult undertaking of transporting, to the banks of the Red river, a large number of men, women and children. The magnitude of the operation would have appalled any less resolute person than Selkirk, but he had experience in emigration, and was provided with means to carry on such a formidable undertaking.

His lordship then issued an advertisement or prospectus which would, in this age of land advertisements, serve as a model. It describes the quantity and cheapness of the lands, and points out that if handled by what is in modern days termed a "syndicate," they would bring hundreds of thousands of pounds by retailing in small lots, at an advance price, to actual settlers, but owing to its remoteness the whole tract is offered for the lump sum of £10,000. The title is stated to be unexceptionable, but the situation such that immediate settlement must not be looked for, and that reason is given why the price demanded is so low. It is proposed, as an alternative, to form a joint stock company, with a capital stock of £20,000, which will sell land to actual settlers at reasonable figures. No Americans are to be accepted as settlers, but special inducements are offered to people from the highland of Scotland, and some parts of Ireland, so that they will not be lost to the Empire by emigration. Religion is not made the ground of disqualification, an unreserved participation in every privilege is to be enjoyed by Protestants and Catholics without distinction, and it is proposed that in every parochial division an allotment of land shall be made for the perpetual support of a clergyman of that persuasion which the majority of the inhabitants adhere to. The joint stock company must undertake to provide settlers with passage to the colony at moderate rates, £10 being mentioned as an estimate. Time accomodation is to be allowed to settlers who would likely be asked ten shillings per acre for the land, or a rental of one shilling per annum in perpetuity. The cultivation of hemp will be encouraged as well as the growth of fine wool, the plains affording a fine grass for pasturage, possessed, in a natural state, by no other part of British America. The fleeces f om ten or twelve sheep will pay for the rent of 100 acres. After ten or twelve years the returns to the shareholders may be expected to increase rapidly. "The amount to which the profits may ultimately arise seems almost to baffle imagination upon any principle of calculation which can reasonably be adopted."

Agents were sent to Ireland and the Highlands of Scotland to engage a number of servants, some for the Hudson's Bay Company's service, and others to labor in the colony; these were engaged for a term of three years and to be sent ahead of the settlers to prepare for their reception. They were each to receive, at the expiration of their contracts, 100 acres of land free of cost.

The Hudson's Bay Company appointed Mr. Miles Macdonnell, formerly captain in the British army, to be governor of the district of Assiniboia, at some point in which the settlement was to be formed, and Lord Selkirk also nominated that gentleman to direct the settlers and look after their and his interests.

In the summer of 1811 the party, numbering about 90 persons, of both sexes and all ages, gathered from Ireland and the north of Scotland, were waiting at Stornoway, in the Island of Lewis, ready for embarkation on the ships of the Hudson's Bay Company, which were sent annually to the posts on the shores of Hudson's bay.

THE NORTHWEST COMPANY.

After the conquest of Canada, in 1761, the fur countries to the west of Lake Superior attracted the attention of Montreal merchants, and traders, in a few years, began to penetrate into the almost unknown wilds of the western forests, prairies and lakes. From the days of the intrepid pioneer La Verandrye, the fur trade had been "farmed out" by the French authorities, but with the departed rule vanished the restrictions to the fur trade. Many of the voyageurs and employees of the persons trading in the interior under the French licenses, remained on the plains of the Red and Saskatchewan rivers, in the districts where the trading posts had been situated, having become so accustomed to the wild savage life, and attached to the Indian women with whom they lived, that they preferred to adopt the customs and pursuits of the Indians to returning to their old homes on the St. Lawrence. McKenzie informs us that for some years after the conquest the Indians west of Lake Superior were compelled to go down-to the posts of the Hudson's Bay Co. at the Bay to obtain their supplies of manufactured goods, the trade from Canada being suspended. It was not until 1766 that the first trader, under the new order of affairs, arrived at the Kaministiquia river. The next year Thomas Curry pushed into the interior, with four canoes laden with goods intended for the Indian trade, and managed to reach the Saskatchewan, from whence he returned the following spring with a large quantity of fine furs. Within a few years a number of traders were competing for the furs secured by the Indians of the Saskatchewan and Athabasca, which trade had, for some years previously, been carried to York Factory on the Hudson Bay. The Hudson's Bay Co. were compelled to take action, and for the first time since their arrival in the Bay, in 1670, after securing their charter, they established a post in the interior. On their account in 1774, Samuel Hearne, who afterward explored north from Churchill to the

Arctic Ocean, erected a fort at Sturgeon Lake, an expansion of the Saskatchewan, where ever since the company has maintained an establishment. When the Montreal traders shortly after this time visited the Red and Assiniboine rivers, they found many French half-breeds, who claimed that the country belonged to them as successors of their Indian mothers. The traders were compelled to pay tribute before they were allowed to barter. In 1781 some traders at Portage la Prairie, while preparing their wintering houses, were attacked by the Crees and Assiniboines, but with the loss of three men they drove off the Indians, killing fifteen warriors and wounding many others. The post was hastily abandoned. The year before the Indians, during a drunken squabble with the traders, assembled at the Eagle Hills, on the Saskatchewan, had forced the whites to fly, after several on both sides had been killed. The smallpox appeared in 1781 amongst the Indians all over the Northwest, and thousands of the natives perished during that and the succeeding year, completely ruining the fur trade, and though they had been reduced to two parties the traders suffered great loss. In 1778 a trader named Peter Pond represented a joint stock company and traded in the Athabasca country with such success that he could find transport to Lake Superior for only one-half of his furs the following spring, but relying on the honesty of the natives he left the balance stored in his wintering house, where, on his return the next season, he found them intact. His success led, in 1783-4, to the formation of the original Northwest Company, the merchants interested dividing the stock into sixteen shares. Some traders, not satisfied with their allotment, formed another company, in which was interested Alexander Mackenzie. These two interests competed for the trade, and rivalry led to such hostile conduct that the result was murder and violence, which terminated in the union of the companies in July, 1787. The gross venture in 1788 amounted to £40,000, covered by 22 shares. In 1798, a new arrangement was entered into, the number of shares being increased to 42, but some of the old partners were dissatisfied and formed a new company called the X Y, of which Sir Alexander McKenzie and Edward Ellice were the chief members. The rivalry between these companies, from 1798 to 1804, was very great, especially on the Red and Assiniboine rivers, but in the latter year an amalgamation was effected. Alexander Henry, in his unpublished journal, on the 1st January, 1805, writes at Pembina, where he was the resident agent of the Northwest company, "It was high time for amalgamation, as every Indian on the river was a chief, and goods were given gratis, except silver works, strouds, and blankets. All the

Indians wore scarlet coats and had large kegs and flasks."

A manuscript inventory of the Northwest Company, now in the archives of the Manitoba Historical Society, shows that the company had for principal posts, in the year 1798, throughout the country west of Lake Superior, the following situations: Grand Portage (Lake Superior), Fort Charlotte (9 miles west of Grand Portage) Pembina River, Rainy Lake, English River, Upper Fort Des Prairies, Fort St. Louis, Cumberland House (the three last on the Saskatchewan), Fort Dauphin, Swan River, Athabasca, Churchill River, Red River, Lake Winnipeg, Slave Lake, and several posts in what is now Minnesota. The total amount of the inventories amounted to £44,819.

It is to be noticed that the Assiniboine, though called so by the Indians from Assine (stone) and boine, or poille (Sioux Indian), was known to the early French traders as the St. Charles, and to the Hudson's Bay Company and Northwest Company employes as the Upper Red River. The Selkirk settlers refer to the river as the Oenaboine. There were a large number of trading posts on the Assiniboine at the beginning of the present century—many more than on the Red River.

This, then, was the condition of affairs on the Red River. The Northwest Company had a number of posts, their employes being principally French Canadians and French half-breeds, and were opposed in the fur trade by the Hudson's Bay Company, who, in the words of Henry, always followed and never led them. Their traders were scattered over the Northwest from Lake Superior to the Pacific where the adventurous McKenzie had led them. They, following in the footsteps of their French predecessors and extending their territories, claimed by right of discovery, the privilege of trading in the land that had remained for long years in their undisputed possession. The Hudson's Bay Co. while claiming the whole of the lands to the head waters of the streams flowing through any connections into Hudson Bay, had never ventured to make good their claim by establishing trading stations in this vast country. At the date the Hudson's Bay Co. sent Mr. Hearne to build Cumberland House, their first inland post, the Montreal traders were in full possession of the interior trade, while a period of forty years had elapsed since the French Canadians under LaVerandrye had planted their forts on Lake Winnipeg and its tributary streams. Though rivals in trade the officers and men of the two companies were on good terms; in many cases, on the Saskatchewan, one enclosure surrounding the buildings of both, only a fence or wall separating the portion assigned to each. Dances and other jollifications were given by the presiding officer in either division of the fort, and the amusements were participated in by the united population. To give some idea of the number of persons housed within the walls of such a fort as I have described I extract from Henry's journal that at the White Mud River House, on the North Saskatchewan, in 1810, the Northwest Company had 28 men, 35 women and 72 children, 135 in all, while their neighbors of the Hudson's Bay Company numbered 85 souls. It is interesting to note that amongst the above-mentioned Northwest people were to be found the names of Le Pierrie, Cardinalle, Succier, Dumont, Des Noyer, Nadeau, Deschamps and Parenteau. I believe all these names are to be found amongst the French Metis of to-day.

When Lord Selkirk began to arrange for the planting of a settlement on the banks of the Red River, the partners of the Northwest Company, resident in England, protested against such a course, and placed every obstacle in their power in the way of his Lordship, to prevent the carrying out of his scheme. They acknowledged that they had purchased Hudson's Bay Company stock within forty-eight hours of the general meeting at which the governor and committee announced the bestowal of the land grant of Assiniboia to Lord Selkirk, and admit it was done as a means to give them an opportunity to protest against the grant. They claimed that Lord Selkirk's object in forming such a colony on the Red River was to break up their fur trade and intercept them in their passage from Canada to the Athabasca and Pacific coast. They denied the rights of exclusive trade advanced by the Hudson's Bay Company, and the legality of the charter of 1670, holding that the French had possessed the country before the conquest, and that after 1761 all British subjects came into possession of the privileges enjoyed by the French traders. They then, after obtaining legal opinions, like Selkirk, from eminent British authorities, informed both the British Government and the Hudson's Bay Company that they were determined to maintain their rights and possessions, while they did not acknowledge the power of jurisdiction or exclusive rights claimed by the Hudson's Bay Co., and would not do so, until they received from the government "a distinct intimation that these rights were recognized and admitted by government, and they would resist any attempts to seize their property or persons, or to dispossess them of their trade, under these pretences."

This was the position assumed by the Northwest Co. when the first party of the Selkirk settlers gathered at Stornoway, in July, 1811.

THE COLONY GOVERNOR.

Documents published by the Canadian archives office, inform us that Miles Macdonell, who was appointed by Lord Selkirk as Governor of the colony, was born in Inverness, Scotland, in 1767. He in after years served as ensign in America in the King's Royal Regiment of New York, returning to Scotland in 1788, where he married. In 1794 he was appointed lieutenant in the second battalion of Royal Canadian Volunteers, to which his father, John Macdonell, Speaker of the Assembly of Upper Canada, had been gazetted as captain. Two years later he received his commission as captain, and from 1800 to 1802 was stationed at Fort George (Niagara). On the reduction of the force he lived in Glengarry, part of his correspondence being dated at Cornwall. Some of his grandchildren are now residing at Brockville, Ont. He died at Point Fortune on the Ottawa in 1828. This was the man chosen by Lord Selkirk to undertake the difficult task of superintending the removal of the colonists to the prairies of the Red River Valley. His experience in the wilds of Canada served him in good stead later on.

Lord Selkirk, in 1810, wrote to Canada urging him to proceed to London, where he would give him an appointment, the nature of which he could not then communicate. Capt. Macdonell went to join his lordship and was immediately placed in charge of the expedition.

THE COLONISTS EMBARK.

The colony servants and employes had assembled at Stornoway to the number of 125, having been engaged in Ireland, the Highlands of Scotland, the Orkneys, Glasgow and London. Most of these persons were engaged as clerks and mechanics for Lord Selkirk and the Hudson's Bay Co.'s service, and it must be understood that, as a rule in the after proceedings the Company's business matters and those of Selkirk's colony were kept entirely distinct from each other.

The following information is extracted from letters of Capt. Macdonell to Lord Selkirk, which have only been made public within this month.

A great deal of difficulty was experienced in getting the people on board the ships, which were the Prince of Wales, the Eddystone, and the Edward and Anne. Macdonell had to apply to the captain of the convoy for a party of marines, and it was necessary to go through the ceremony of having some impressed and put on board that man-of-war, which was to accompany them to Hudson's Bay. One man had enlisted with a military recruiting party, but he was taken from the soldiers and shipped. Five absconded, and were not recovered. While the captain of the Edward and Anne was on shore making his clearance from the custom house, a Captain McKenzie, who had been agent for the Hudson's Bay Company at Stornoway the year before, boarded the vessel with a recruiting party and gave enlisting money to some of the men, but he

and the soldiers were ejected from the ship without the recruits. McKenzie then awaited the arrival of the collector of customs and claimed some of the men, but was not allowed to take them. On this vessel were men from Glasgow, Ireland, and a few from Orkney, numbering in all 76. After mustering the passengers the collector of customs (whose wife was an aunt of Sir Alexander McKenzie) read the clause of the Emigration Act regulating the provisions for passengers, and a public declaration made, that if any were unwilling to go abroad they might go to the shore. Several said they were not willing—many went over the ship's side into McKenzie's boat—one party ran away with the ship's boat, but was brought back—one man jumped into the sea and swam for it until he was picked up by the recruiting boat. The revenue cutter's boat was likewise engaged in taking the unwilling, and to cap the troubles of Macdonell, the collector took ashore a number in his own boat. Macdonell could not see clearly if the fact of the men being indentured servants excluded them from the action of emigration act, and so refrained from following them to compel them to reship. He blamed Mr. Reid, the collector, for all the trouble, and claimed that person was influenced in his conduct by Sir Alexander McKenzie and other interested persons of the Northwest company resident in England.

ARRIVAL AT YORK FACTORY.

At length on the 26th July the ships set sail for York Factory, Hudson Bay, with 105 persons engaged for colony work and for the fur trade of the Hudson's Bay Co., 90 of whom were workmen and 15 clerks. Some of the Irishmen were turbulent during the early part of the voyage, but the men from Glasgow gave the most trouble of all. The voyage covered 61 days and Macdonell writes that it was the longest ever known, stormy weather on the ocean being followed by fine mild weather with moderate winds when the bay was entered. The ships' captains were incompetent, and the Edward and Anne was wretchedly fitted for the voyage. The colonists experienced fairly good health and were drilled with arms, few of them knowing how to fire off a gun. The effects of the deserters at Stornoway were auctioned off, and brought £27 sterling. Messrs. Auld (superintendent) and Cook (governor at York Factory) afforded the party every assistance on their arrival and informed Macdonell that a great number of the Hudson's Bay Company's officers and men were interested in the success of the colony, and were looking forward to joining it on their retirement from the service. Orders had been sent to Red River to secure provisions for the people on their arrival there in the following spring, the season being too far advanced to allow of their going on that autumn. Macdonell had foreseen this delay. News had been received that the Red River had overflowed its banks in the spring, a circumstance said to be a new experience in that country.

ARTILLERY.

Two old iron swivel guns had been taken from the stores of Lord Seaforth at Stornoway, but Capt. Macdonald, not satisfied with them, asked for some "sound brass pieces," 3-pounders, with carriages, etc., complete. Without doubt these guns were sent, and transported to Red river, for carriages in a state of decay and bearing that date are still to be seen about the old buildings of Fort Garry. A few years after, the Northwest Company took possession of nine cannon stored in the warehouse of Lord Selkirk at what was termed the "Government House," which a few months later became Fort Douglas. These cannon played a very prominent part in the history of the Selkirk settlement from 1811 to as late a date as 1870, when Riel, as President of the Provisional Government, commanded the situation largely through being in possession of them. They are now scattered, most of them being in the custody of private individuals who use them to adorn their lawns, or have consigned them to the lumber heaps of their back yards.

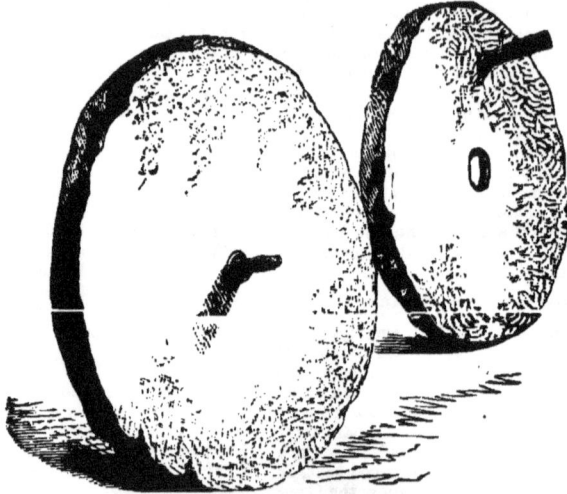

SELKIRK GRINDSTONES.

THE FIRST GRIST MILL.

The stores intended for the settlement were placed in the York Factory warehouse, and mention is made by Macdonell of the grindstones, some of which had, by an error, been left on board the ships. It is very probable, however, that the old-fashioned grindstone now in possession of the Manitoba Historical society, a cut of which is herewith shown, was one of the identical stock landed that year. Each half is about two feet in diameter and an inch and a half thick. One stone being placed on the other, the primitive handle was grasped by the operator and the upper stone turned round smartly, as the grain was poured into the hole in the centre about the pivot pin, the flour produced gradually working outward between the stones. While a slow and laborious process, in comparison with the roller system of this day, many a bushel of wheat was, by the exercise of patience and muscle, run through this old-fashioned mill, and furnished a strong and wholesome food to the colonists.

WINTERING AT YORK FACTORY.

This first party of colonists was sent from York Factory over to the Nelson River, near Flamboro Head, where huts were erected for their accommodation, and a new winter road cut out, reducing the distance from 28 to 23 miles. The rations issued daily comprised from one to two pounds of venison, when obtainable, and a pint of oatmeal, with an occasional allowance of pease, barley and molasses. Bacon appears on the requisitions drawn on the York storehouse, but it was not used where fresh meat was procurable. Scurvy soon appeared, and on the 21st January, 1812, 23 men were down with it, but the extensive use of spruce juice almost entirely removed the evil.

By the 26th October the people moved into the houses, which were built of logs, with clay and moss-covered roofs. Plenty of boards were obtained from an abandoned house of the company on the opposite or southern side of the Nelson River, not far from Flamboro Head, so that comfortable bunks and floors were constructed. Two fences were erected, for a couple of miles in extent, on each side of the river, with snares placed in them for the purpose of catching deer, which, however, did not arrive that fall as was usual, but in March and April a very large number were captured in the snares, thousands crossing the river in the early part of May. Supplies of provisions were hauled on sleds from York Factory each week, and, though the weather at times was most severe, no accidents from freezing happened. Macdonnell had hired a man named Will Finlay at York in the autumn, he being a discharged company's servant. This man gave a great deal of trouble to Macdonnell, for he instigated some of the turbulent ones to resist all authority and to refuse to do any work.

On New Year's day some of the Irishmen made a violent attack on the Orkneymen, three of whom were so brutally beaten that their lives were despaired of for a month afterward. The trouble arose from the fact that a pint of rum had been served out to each individual with which to celebrate the day.

In February Finlay, who would not obey orders and refused to do any work, was removed to a hut built for the purpose of confining him in, but on the first night he occupied it thirteen men of the party assembled and burnt the hut to the ground amidst wild shouts of defiance.

The insurgents were summoned to appear before Mr. Hillier, a magistrate who accompanied the colonists, and Capt. Macdonnell. Nine of these people were Glasgow men and the remaining four were young Orkney lads who had been induced to join them. At the examination they refused to submit to the authority of the magistrates and contemptuously walked away, claiming that they were not being treated according to the promises made them by the agent at the time of engaging. These malcontents were given the choice between starving and hauling their own provisions from York Factory, and were notified that they would be sent back to Scotland for trial. In the spring they obtained possession of firearms, but Mr. Auld, the superintendent of the Hudson's Bay Company ejected them from the fort, and refused to give them any provisions until they surrendered their arms and submitted, which they did shortly after, and being separated went to work, and it was decided not to return them to Scotland, as their reports would have the effect of preventing the enlisting of men for the service.

Four new boats were built at York during the winter, after the batteau pattern, though much difficulty was experienced in getting the Company's people to depart from their regular models, which Macdonnell claimed were not nearly so good, being only 22 feet in the keel, while his were 28 feet long.

An Irish priest from Killala named Bourke was the only clergyman with the party, but he returned to Ireland, from York, after spending the winter with Capt. Macdonnell, who considered that while he might make a good recruiting agent for the colony in Ireland, did not think "he would ever make a convert to the Catholic religion." Macdonnell was anxious to have a priest sent out, who would be well recommended, but makes no allusion to supplying a Presbyterian minister for the people of that denomination, and who were expected to be in the great majority in the future colony.

In writing Selkirk from York, Macdonnell presses on His Lordship the necessity of having martial law established in Assiniboia, for, "within the tract all traders must take out a license, which may answer a good purpose with the Northwest Co." He proposed to organize a company of fifty men at the first outset, the troops to be mounted so as to act as infantry or cavalry as the service might require.

It is probable that the number of this first party under Macdonnell has heretofore been over-estimated by historians, for while most writers on the subject mention 70 as the number, it is stated by Macdonnell in a letter to Lord Selkirk, dated 4th July, 1812, at York Factory, " 22 is my portion out of 49, all that are effective of last year's importation. The people are so fluctuating that I cannot yet send a list of my party. A man of one nation is prejudiced against ‛going with one of another. I shall go on with any number, take possession of the tract and hoist the standard." He left on the 5th July for the Red River.

It was about August or Sept., 1812, that these pioneers arrived at the Red River and began the erection of dwellings and storehouses on the west bank, about three-quarters of a mile north of the mouth of the Assiniboine; previous to which, however, Governor Macdonnell ordered all his people to assemble, and read his commission as Lord Selkirk's representative and governor. Ellice writes that a salute was fired at the Hudson's Bay fort in the neighborhood, the Indians assembled looking on in silent wonder.

Though every exertion was put forth to prepare for the approaching winter, it appears that some of the party were compelled to live with the freemen in the neighborhood, and the North-West Company's employees rendered great assistance to them, furnishing goods and provisions ‚for their support. In the spring of 1813 Governor Macdonnell also procured from the North-Westers, potatoes, barley, oats, garden seeds, four cows, a bull, pigs, fowls, etc., articles which the traders could ill afford to spare, though at each of their posts on the Red river a quantity of vegetables were raised for their own use.

A small party of colonists arrived at York Factory in the autumn of 1812, and worked through to the settlement the next year. There was a strong spirit of insubordination exhibited by these people on the voyage to York Factory and a conspiracy was entered into to seize the vessel and sell her in some foreign country. The captain armed his men and with the assistance of some cannon loaded with grape shot subdued the uprising. Most of these emigrants were engaged as laborers and servants, and came from Scotland and Ireland. Several families were in the party.

Finding, on their arrival at the settlement on the Red river, that it would be impossible to provide provisions for them during the following winter, the colonists were sent up the Red river to the mouth of the Pembina, where on the south side, they erected huts and enclosed them with palisades. This place was named Fort Daer, after Lord Selkirk, who was Baron Daer. Here they had their headquarters, though many of them were forced to join with the plain hunters engaged in killing buffalo to supply the trading posts. The hardships endured by some were extreme, and as they were not provided with horses the stalking of buffalo for their subsistence was a dangerous and precarious mode of hunting.

The journals of the Northwesters, at the various posts, contain many notes of the supplies and assistance afforded to even the employees of the Hudson's Bay Company in the early days of this country, and it may well be imagined that the colonists, unaccustomed to the life and climate and not properly clad in suitable garments, suffered intensely. In reviewing fairly the events that succeeded this generous conduct of the Northwesters, it will add to one's perception of the true situation, if these acts are not lost sight of, for many outrageous charges have been preferred against the people of the Northwest company.

The colonists who wintered at Pembina returned to the colony in the spring and continued their efforts to cultivate the clearings near the bank of the river. Much of what is now open land or prairie, was at that date covered with timber or scrubby bushes. There seems to be no doubt that Lord Selkirk, or his managers, were somewhat negligent in not providing horses for the settlers to work their farms. Horses were to be had in plenty from the Assiniboine and other Indians, for the Northwesters for fifteen years previous had obtained and regularly used horses at their establishments, and the free hunters were equally well supplied. The colonists were compelled to break the ground with hoes and clear away the scrub as best they could.

In the early part of this year (1814) a large number of emigrants sent out by Lord Selkirk the previous summer, arrived at the Red River settlement. They had been landed at Churchill on the 13th August after an eventful voyage, during which fever raged on board. They were sent up the Churchill River about fifteen miles, where log houses were erected and to this place during the winter their rations were drawn on flat sleds from the fort. Owing to some disagreement about hunting grouse, which were abundant during the winter, Mr. Auld, the officer of the Hudson's Bay Company, demanded and obtained the locks from the guns owned by the colonists, and they were unable to lay in stores of these birds.

After a severe winter the larger portion of the party were sent to York Factory, leaving Churchill in April. All their provisions and baggage had to be drawn by themselves on sleds, snowshoes being in general use. At York they arrived, after suffering terribly, and were then established in huts, after which time, the spring opening, they obtained an abundance of fresh venison and feathered game, upon which they principally subsisted until they started on the voyage up the rivers to Lake Winnipeg and on to the colony settlement, after having been joined by the remainder of the party, consisting chiefly of elderly persons who had been carried by boats from Churchill to York later in the spring.

The population of the settlement was now about two hundred, and another addition was made to it the next year (1815), the circumstances relating to which will be dealt with later on, as it is here necessary to notice the first occasion on which the Northwest Co. and Governor Macdonnell came into conflict.

On the 8th of January, 1814, Macdonnell issued a proclamation, which, after reciting the fact that the Hudson's Bay Co. had ceded to Lord Selkirk the territory of Assiniboia, and that his Lordship had duly appointed Miles Macdonnell to be governor of the same, continued as follows: "And whereas, the welfare of the families at present forming settlements on the Red River within the said territory, with those on their way to it, passing the winter at York or Churchill Forts, in Hudson's Bay, as also those who are expected to arrive next autumn, renders it a necessary and indispensable part of my duty to provide for their support. In the yet uncultivated state of the country, the ordinary resources derived from the buffalo and other wild animals hunted within the said territory, are not deemed more than adequate for the requisite supply; wherefore it is hereby ordered that no person trading in furs or provisions within the territory for the Honourable Hudson's Bay Company, the North-West Company, or any individual or unconnected traders or persons whatever, shall take out any provisions, either of flesh, dried meat, grain or vegetables, procured or raised within the said territory, by land or water carriage, for one twelve months from the date hereof, save and except what may be judged necessary for the trading parties at this present within the territory to carry them to their respective destinations, and who may on due application to me obtain a license for the same. The provisions procured and raised as above shall be taken for the use of the colony, and that no loss may accrue to the parties concerned they will be paid for by British bills at the customary rates. And be it hereby further made known, that whosoever shall be detected in attempting to convey out, or shall aid or assist in conveying out, or attempting to carry out, any provisions prohibited as above, either by land or water carriage, shall be taken into custody and prosecuted as the laws in such cases direct, and the provisions so taken, as well as any goods or chattels of what nature soever, which may be taken along with them, and also the craft, carriages and cattle, instrumental in conveying away the same, to any part but the settlement on Red River, shall be forfeited.

Given under my hand at Fort Daer, (Pembina), the 8th day of January, 1841.

[Signed.]   MILES MACDONNELL,
                                        Governor.
By order of the Governor.
[Signed.]   JOHN SPENCER,
                                        Secretary.

To understand what would be the effect of the carrying out of the terms of this proclamation to the Northwest company, it is necessary to be aware of the fact that a large number of hunters were kept at their Red River and Assiniboine posts, to capture buffalo , and make the dried meat and pemican which was shipped to Lake Winnipeg to provision the army of boatmen engaged in carrying out to Lake Superior the produce of the winter's trade throughout the whole vast country west and north, extending even to the Pacific ocean, and also to return the incoming crews in the autumn to the upper stations. This supply of provisions once cut off the fur trade of the Northwest Company would be destroyed or carried on only at and immense an ruinous expediture of capital.

Governor Macdonnell took immediate steps to follow up his proclamation by seizing provision-stores of the Northwest Company, and trouble ensued which led to open antagonism between the rival interests.

THE TROUBLES COMMENCE.

The proclamation of Governor Macdonnell was posted throughout the district and also notices of it served on the officers in charge of the posts of the Northwest Company.

On the 15th March, 1814, a party of men at the Selkirk establishment was detailed to enforce the provisions of the proclamation. Arms were served out by John

Spencer, who had been appointed sheriff by Governor Macdonnell, and the detachment was sent to the plain south of Pembina, near Turtle River, where a band of Freemen had accumulated a quantity of pemican and dried meat. When this armed body arrived on the scene (it will be noticed that no attention was paid to the fact that this place was in the United States) the Freemen were disposing of these provisions to some traders in the service of the Northwest Co. A Mr. Warren and Michael Macdonnell had charge of the Selkirk people, and they at once ordered their men to fix bayonets and load their muskets with ball cartridge. This done they by force seized the provisions and took them to the Selkirk Settlement.

Again on the 5th of June Sheriff Spencer, with an armed force, proceeded to Brandon House, an establishment of the Northwest Co., and after cutting down some palisades entered the fort, broke open the doors of the warehouse and seized 605 packages of pemican and other provisions, the product of the past season's hunt, which it was intended to transport to Lake Winnipeg and elsewhere to feed the voyageurs from the vast inland districts en route to Fort William.

It was for these acts of violence, the first which occurred in the district, that Gov. Miles Macdonnell and his sheriff, John Spencer, were afterwards arrested and sent down to Canada for trial under a warrant issued by A. N. McLeod, a justice of the peace for the Indian Territory, and a partner of the Northwest Company.

A few weeks after the seizure of the provisions, the traders of the Northwest Company began to arrive from the detached posts, only to find that no rations remained to accompany their brigades of boats to Fort William. Instead of asserting their superiority by force of arms, they quitely conferred with Governor Macdonnell, and agreed to return during the next winter any quantity of provisions he would then give them to enable them to proceed to Lake Superior. Macdonnell accordingly handed over some of their own pemican, and they went on their journey to the great gathering of the Northwest Company, which took place annually at Fort William. Certainly the Northwesterns restrained their natural feelings in a wonderful manner in acting so moderately as they did under the circumstances.

THE NORTHWESTERS DETERMINE TO RESIST.

At the annual meeting of the partners at Fort William, it was decided to resist all future attempts of Gov. Macdonnell in interrupting the trade of the Northwest Company, and evidently they also arranged a scheme which, if successfully carried out, would break up the Selkirk colony by depopulating it. Duncan Cameron was sent to take charge of the Northwest Co's interests at Ft. Gibraltar, on the Red River, and Alexander McDonell was despatched in a like capacity to Brandon Brandon House and the Qu'Appelle river establishments.

Arriving in August, 1814, at their posts they learned that in June, Governor Macdonnell had sent a party of 25 men, armed with muskets and bayonets, up the Assiniboine river, one day's journey from the colony, where, in expectation that the Northwest Co. would send down provisions by boats, they camped and planted a loaded cannon on the bank to force a surrender of the stores. They succeeded a few days afterwards in seizing 90 sacks of pemican, the property of the North Westers, and in capturing some employees, who were taken as prisoners to the settlement, but soon released. On this occasion some of the Selkirk people refused to

strange that from the moment they arrived at York Factory this tale of the Indians attacking them had been dinned into their ears, first by the servants of the Hudson's Bay Co. (as written by Governor Macdonnell himself), and at this time by the Northwest people. The truth is, that the Indians were almost from the first extremely friendly to the settlers, hunting for them and later on offering to fight for them if necessary.

GOVERNOR MACDONNELL ISSUES PROCLAMATIONS.

But Cameron was not allowed to thus entice away the colonists without resistance from Governor Macdonnell, who closely guarded the interests of his noble patron. On the 21st of October, 1814, two months after Cameron's arrival, Macdonnell issued and served the following notice:

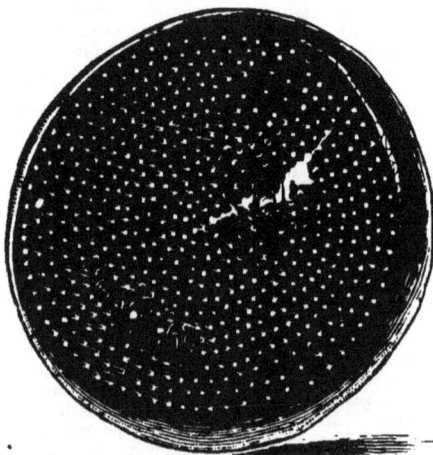

SELKIRK SIEVE, OF RAWHIDE, FOR CLEANING WHEAT

act as constables, giving as a reason that the North Westers had saved them from starving after their arrival at the settlement, and they were not going to make such a poor return.

DUNCAN CAMERON.

Duncan Cameron was, as I am informed by a Selkirk settler still living, "a fine old gentleman," much liked by the settlers. He at once after his arrival ingratiated himself with the Selkirk settlers, invited them to dine with him, and during the winter, by promises of lands and employment for them in Canada, he succeeded in inducing a number to consent to abandon the colony, and accept the offer made by the Northwest Co., of a free passage. It is alleged that he also frightened the settlers by pretending that he had information that the Indians would attack them during the next summer if they remained. It was a hard trial for the settlers, and it is

"DISTRICT OF ASSINIBOIA.

"To Duncan Cameron, acting for the Northwest company at the forks of the Red river :

"Take notice that by the authority and on the behalf of your landlord, the Right Hon. Thomas, Earl of Selkirk, I do hereby warn you, and all your associates of the Northwest company, to quit the post and premises you now occupy at the forks of the Red river within six calendar months from the date hereof."

Similar notices were served on the other Northwest Company's officers in charge of posts, and a very bitter feeling engendered in consequence. Towards spring several collisions took place between the men of the two companies, each side claiming to be innocent of the charges made by the other.

THE SETTLERS SEIZE SELKIRK'S CANNON.

Duncan Cameron had arrested Sheriff

Spencer in the autumn and sent him down to Rainy Lake, and on the 3rd April, 1815, during the temporary absence of Miles Macdonnell from the settlement, he notified Archibald McDonald, who was acting for the governor, to hand over to the settlers the cannon "which had already been employed to disturb the peace of his Majesty's loyal subjects in this quarter," not with a view of making any hostile use of them, but to place them out of harm's way. He had by this time seduced the majority of the settlers from Gov. Macdonnell, and on leaving this matter to them, the next morning they broke open the Selkirk warehouse and forcibly took possession of the nine cannon stored there, and drew them on sleds to Fort Gibraltar. On Gov. Macdonnell's return, which was shortly after the seizure of the cannon, he issued a warrant to search for and recover the stolen property, but Cameron would only permit

ern Canada, where many of their descendants may now be found, residing principally in the counties of Elgin and Middlesex.

After their departure the Northwesters so worked on the fears of the remaining settlers, numbering about fifty, that they became discouraged. Lord Selkirk's friends have stated that their horses were stolen, cattle driven away and their persons threatened with violence, so that about the 25th of June (1815) most of them embarked in their boats and proceeded down the Red River and across Lake Winnipeg to Jack Fish River (now Norway House) where they remained until August, when they were joined by Colin Robertson and twenty voyageurs sent by Lord Selkirk from Montreal to assist the colonists.

SOME COLONISTS RETURN.

They returned to their old home on the 19th August, when they found that most of

FORT DOUGLAS.

four of the searching party to enter Fort Gibraltar and then refused to allow a search to be made, enforcing his refusal by arming his men to resist. Then a large number of the Selkirk colonists deserted the settlement and went over to the Northwest fort, and when one of their number was arrested by the Governor's warrant, the deserters, with the Northwest servants, rescued him by force.

GOVERNOR MACDONNELL ARRESTED.

A series of petty hostilities were engaged in during the next month, and Governor Macdonnell was finally arrested under the warrant issued by A. N. McLeod the autumn previous, and carried down to Montreal for trial, but on his arrival there the partners of the Northwest Co. decided not to prosecute him and he was liberated.

SELKIRK COLONISTS ABANDON THE SETTLEMENT.

In June 140 of the Selkirk colonists packed up and were transported by the Northwest Company free of charge to West-

their houses had been destroyed. They re-occupied the remaining dwellings and exerted themselves to build anew as well as gather in the crops left standing, which luckily had been preserved by the Hudson's Bay Co.'s men, who remained on the spot to look after the trading interests of the Company. Over 1500 bushels of wheat, some other grain, and a large stock of potatoes were housed. It was at this time that the site of the residence of the Selkirk governor, with the buildings about it, was named Fort Douglas, after his lordship.

THE FOURTH PARTY OF EMIGRANTS.

Lord Selkirk's agents were working in Sutherlandshire, Scotland, and in the spring of 1815 a large party of emigrants had been secured, the majority of them hailing from the Parish of Kildonan. Some of these people had sufficient ready money to pay over to his lordship the sum of £10 for passage to the Red river. Others, not so fortunate, agreed to engage as servants for the colony

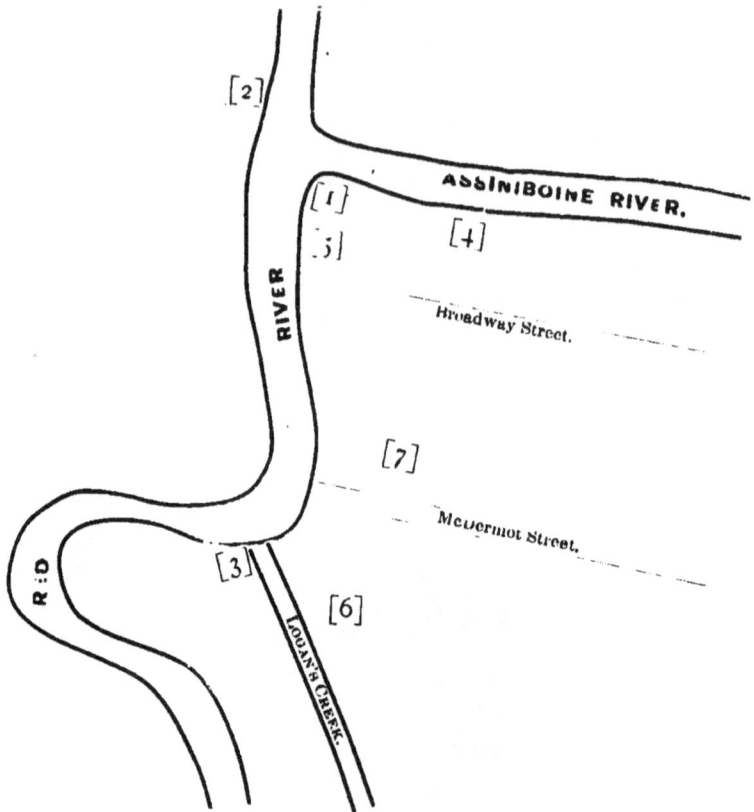

KEY.

1. Fort Rouge—built by LaVerandrye about 1736.

   The Forks—built by Northwest Company about 1803.

   Fort Gibraltar—built by Northwest Company about 1806.

   Destroyed by Lord Selkirk's agents in 1816. Rebuilt by Northwest Company about 1817; occupied by H. B. Co. after amalgamation with Northwest Company in 1821 and on April 18th, 1822, its name was changed by Sir Geo. Simpson, the H. B. Co. governor, to Fort Garry.

   Fort Garry, a new fort built by Governor Pelly, but destroyed by the great flood of 1826. It was rebuilt by Governer Pelly in 1826, and afterwards was used as buildings for a model farm.

2. H. B. Co's store, for, perhaps fort. In use prior to arrival of Selkirk colonists in 1812.

3. Government House of the Selkirk Colony, afterwards (in the fall of 1815) it was named Fort Douglas. 1812-1826.

4. The last Fort Garry built by Governor Christie in 1835-36.

5. Stables built for model farm about 1840.

6. Grove of trees beside present residence of Ex-Mayor Logan, where Governor Semple and his party were buried after the Seven Oakes tragedy in June, 1816.

7. Hudson's Bay Company's fort partly built by Peter Fidler in 1817, and finished by James Sutherland in 1819. It was situated between McDermot and Notre Dame street east, a few hundred yards back from the bank of the Red River. It was in use certainly in 1821, Joseph Bird being the chief factor in charge.

until such time as they could pay off their indebtedness on this score. About seventy-two persons embarked at Stromness on board the Hedlow, which set sail on June 17, 1815, in company with two ships of the Hudson's Bay Co., all the vessels being under the care of a sloop of war to protect them from the French privateers. The colonists were accompanied by James Sutherland, who, previous to their departure, had been an elder in the Established Church of Scotland, and had been duly licensed to marry, baptise, and perferm the duties of a preacher and spiritual guide to the colonists. He remained at the settlement for two or three years and removed to Canada. Landing at York Factory on the 18th August, they immediately after set out on the arduous voyage of some 700 miles to the colony, which place they reached on the 5th of November.

GOVERNOR SEMPLE.

With this last-mentioned party of settlers came Robert Semple, who had, under a new arrangement for conducting their business in the territories, been appointed governor in chief by the Hudson's Bay Co. He was from all accounts a most amiable man and a warm friend of the colonists, whose interests he looked after to the best of his ability under the distressing circumstance that provisions were scarce and difficult to obtain. The colonists were again compelled to proceed to Fort Daer (Pembina) to winter, and on their arrival there found that the buffalo were far distant. Many of them proceeded on over a hundred miles during the early winter to the locality where the Freemen and Indians were hunting the buffalo. A miserable winter was passed by the poor people, who, of course, were of little service in their new occupation of running the bison. Once more the Metis and Indian extended their hospitality to the suffering colonists.

Colin Robertson had been selected by Lord Selkirk to organize an expedition to the Athabasca in 1815, and that gentleman proceeded to Montreal and secured a large number of voyageurs to accompany him to that remote district, which was outside the bounds of the territory claimed by the Hudson's Bay Company as their exclusive preserve. The object of this move was to compete with the Northwest Co. in the fur trade of those regions, and if possible ruin them. This once gained, the fur trade of the whole Northwest would practically be left in their hands. Colin Robertson, however, only accompanied his brigade as far as Lake Winnipeg, where he met the Selkirk colonists evicted by Duncan Cameron and his men. He at once returned to the Red River with the colonists, as mentioned above, leaving the Athabasca expedition to proceed on its way. Of this ill-fated expedition it is only necessary to say here that no preparation having been

made for their reception at Athabasca, they were reduced to the utmost extremity for food, and while searching for provisions seventeen out of a party of eighteen starved to death. The survivors of the main body, in many cases, owed their lives to assistance rendered by the North Westers.

SEIZURE OF DUNCAN CAMERON.

Colin Robertson took an active part in the scenes enacted in the settlement during the winter of 1815-16.

In October Robertson made a prisoner of Cameron and took him to Ft. Douglass, at the same time taking possession of Ft. Gibraltar. The charge laid against Cameron was that of having enticed away the colonists in the early part of the summer. Having detained him as a prisoner for some days, and searched his fort for the cannon and arms taken by the colonists from Fort Douglas the previous spring, he was set at liberty. Gunn, in his history of Manitoba, informs us that on this occasion Cameron was horse-whipped while a loaded pistol was held to his head.

In the early part of March, 1816, Govenor Semple left the settlement on a tour of inspection of the posts of the Hudson's Bay Co., situated in the interior, and did not return until some time in June.

CAPTURE OF FORTS GIBRALTAR AND PEMBINA.

As soon as Governor Semple disappeared, Colin Robertson, as acting governor, began to work mischief. On the night of the 17th of March, 1816, he headed an armed party from Fort Douglas, and broke into Fort Gibraltar, where, on entering the master's house, he found Duncan Cameron and his clerks. Making prisoners of them all, Robertson proceeded to remove everything in the establishment down to Fort Douglas, the furs afterward being sent to York Factory. On the 19th of March more men and cannon were placed in the Northwest fort, and, the winter express from the interior posts arriving, it was seized and the letters opened by Robertson. Finding it to be too much trouble to guard so many prisoners, the Selkirk people liberated most of the Northwest Co.'s servants, who, at this most inclement season, had to seek out friends amongst the Freemen on the plains to secure a living.

Three days after this assault at Fort Gibraltar, another armed body of the Selkirk people captured Fort Pembina, taking about ten prisoners and a very large quantity of provisions. At Pembina quantities of potatoes and other field vegetables were cultivated yearly by the Northwest Co. for the use of their posts, their fields having been first cultivated in 1801. The prisoners taken here were sent in bonds to Fort Douglas.

Later on, in April, an attack was made

ou the Northwest Company's fort at the Qu'Appelle River, but Alexander McDonel, who was in charge, gave the beseigers such a hot reception that they retired in bad order.

Though the Northesters had offered no violence during these aggravated attacks of Robertson, Alexander McDonel, always known in the country as "White Headed McDonel," sent word appealing to the distant posts, urging the Northwesters to come to his assistance. He was aware that the guns of Fort Douglas commanded the Red River and his ultimate capture,

at York Cameron was placed on board ship for England, but owing to the lateness of the season had to be taken back to James Bay, where the crew wintered, but proceeded to London in the next summer (1817), where he was set at liberty, without trial, neither party desiring to take the case into an English court on account of the position of affairs at that time. Cameron afterwards returned to Canada.

DESTRUCTION OF FORT GIBRALTAR.

In the early part of April the Selkirk authorities razed Fort Gibraltar to the

A SELKIRK CANNON, SINCE REMOUNTED.

with that of all his provisions and furs, would follow an attempt to descend the Assiniboine from Q'uAppelle, and perceived that it was only by procuring a large force of men to assist him that he could carry his produce through to Fort William in the spring. After gathering a party together he turned the tables on Robertson by capturing some Hudson's Bay Co.'s boats, laden with furs and pemican, as they descended the Assiniboine. Messengers carried news of this event to Fort Douglas and Colin Robertson started for York Factory in a boat, taking with him, as prisoner, Duncan Cameron. It may be here mentioned that on their arrival

ground, carrying away the timbers to Fort Douglas to strengthen that establishment, and fire was set to the remains. To-day, in the river bank, at the point between the Red and Assiniboine rivers, where Fort Gibraltar stood, may be seen the charred wood, ashes and debris of the burnt fort.

In April, also, the colonists returned by river from Pembina, and began the cultivation of their patches of cleared land. It has been frequently referred to that while the colonists were but poorly supplied with agricultural tools, using the hoe instead of the plow, that care had been taken by Selkirk to send along cannon and muskets in abundance.

This was the state of affairs up to the middle of June, 1816, when a most deplorable and atrocious act was committed, which again broke up the colony and sent a score of men to their graves.

THE KILLING OF GOV. SEMPLE AND TWENTY MEN.

On Governor Semple's return to Fort Douglas, from visiting the inland posts of the Hudson's Bay Co., in June, 1816, he again assumed the direction of affairs, which had been temporarily managed by Colin Robertson. That he did not altogether approve of the management during his absence is learned from the testimony of an eye-witness, yet living, in the person of Donald Murray, who informs me that Robertson was in great disfavor with the Settlement and Hudson's Bay Co. officials, and when, on hearing of the probability of an attack by the Northwesters, he started for York Factory in a boat, taking Duncan Cameron, a prisoner, he insultingly hoisted a pemican sack as an ensign instead of the British flag, which was the usual one used on such occasions.

Word was received at the settlement that the Northwesters were determined to destroy both it and the settlers. On the 17th of June, Peguis, chief of the Swampy Indians, residing in the district about the mouth of the Red river, waited on Governor Semple to offer the services of his men, some seventy in number, to assist in protecting the colonists. This proffered assistance was declined with thanks by Semple, who did not foresee the occurrences of the succeeding two days.

Alex. McDonel sent a party of about sixty Canadians and half-breeds with a few Indians, mounted on horseback and bearing some provisions, across by land from the Assiniboine, to the Red river, the route followed taking them along the edge of the swamps, about two miles out on the prairie from Fort Douglas, and from that point gradually drawing nearer to the main highway, which is now the northern continuation of Winnipeg's Main street, until it joined the latter at a spot known as "Seven Oaks," on account of seven oak trees growing there, within a hundred yards or so south of a small coolie, now called Inkster's creek. One half of the Metis had arrived at the coolie and passed on to Frog Plain (Kildonan church prairie), taking two or three settlers prisoners to prevent their giving the alarm, when the remainder were discovered by a sentinel, placed in the watch tower of Fort Douglas, with a telescope. He immediately gave an alarm, and Governor Semple left the fort with a small party of company's servants to intercept the Metis, whom he met at Seven Oaks as they arrived at the highway. Semple had by this time, been joined by some of his servants and officials, so that he arrived on the scene with about 28 companions.

It is difficult to get at the exact truth of what followed this meeting of the rival traders. A host of affidavits are on record made by men on both sides, who, while agreeing in the main particulars, disagree as to details. However, herewith is given a version of the affair emanating from each side.

The first is an affidavit made by John Pritchard, who had been in the service of both the X Y and Northwest companies, but in 1816 was a resident of the Selkirk settlement. He was the father of the Rev. S. Pritchard, and grandfather of the Rev. Canon Matheson, of this city.

"On the afternoon of the 19th of June, 1816, a man in the watch-house called out that the half-breeds were coming. The governor, some other gentlemen and myself looked through spy-glasses, and I distinctly saw some armed people on horseback passing along the plains. A man then called out. 'They (meaning the half-breeds) are making for the settlers,' on which the governor said, 'We must go out and meet these people; let twenty men follow me.' We proceeded down the old road leading down the settlement. As we were going along we met many of the settlers running to the fort, crying, 'The half-breeds! the half-breeds!' When we were advanced about three-quarters of a mile along the settlement, we saw some people on horseback behind a point of woods. On our nearer approach the party seemed more numerous, on which the governor made a halt and sent for a field piece, which, delaying to arrive, he ordered us to advance. We had not proceeded far before the half-breeds, on horseback, with their faces painted in the most hideous manner, and in the dresses of Indian warriors, came forward and surrounded us in the form of a half moon. We then extended our line and moved more into the open plain, and as they advanced we retreated a few steps backward, and then saw a Canadian named Boucher ride up to us waving his hand and calling out, 'What do you want?' The governor replied, 'What do you want?' To which Boucher answered, 'We want our fort.' The governor said, 'Go to your fort.' They were by this time near each other, and consequently spoke too low for me to hear. Being at some little distance to the right of the governor, I saw him take hold of Boucher's gun, and almost immediately a general discharge of fire arms took place, but whether it began on our side, or that of the enemy, it was impossible to distinguish. My attention was then directed towards my personal defence. In a few minutes almost all our people were either killed or wounded. Captain Rogers, having fallen, rose up again and came towards me' when, not seeing one of our party who was not either killed or disabled, I called out to him, 'For God's sake give yourself up!' He ran towards the enemy for that purpose, myself following him. He raised up his hands, and, in English, and broken French, called for mercy. A half-breed (son of Col. William McKay) shot him through the head, and another cut open his belly with a knife with the most horrid imprecations. Fortunately for me, a Canadian (named Lavigne), joining his entreaties to mine, saved me (though with the greatest difficulty) from sharing the fate of my friend at that moment. After this I was reserved from death, in the most providential manner, no less than six different times on my way to and at the Frog Plain (the head-quarters of these cruel murderers), I there saw Alexander Murray and his wife, two of William Bannerman's children and Alexander Sutherland, settlers, and likewise Antony McDonnell, a servant, were prisoners, having been taken before the action took place. With the exception of myself, no quarter was given to any of us. The knife, axe or ball, put a period to the existence of the wounded; and on the bodies of the dead were practiced all those barbarities which characterize the inhuman heart of the savage. The amiable and mild Mr. Semple, lying on his side (his thigh having been broken) and supporting his head upon his hand, addressed the commander of our enemies, by inquiring if he was Mr. Grant; and being answered in the affirmative, 'I am not mortally wounded,' said Mr. Semple; 'and if you get me conveyed to the fort, I think I should live.' Grant promised he would do so, and immediately left him in the care of a Canadian, who afterwards told that an Indian of their party came up and shot Mr. Semple in the breast. I entreated Grant to procure me the watch, or even the seals, of Mr. Semple, for the purpose of transmitting them to his friends, but I did not succeed. Our force amounted to twenty-eight persons, of whom twenty-one were killed and one wounded, the governor, Captain Rogers, Mr. James White, surgeon, Mr. Alexander McLean, settler, Mr. Wilkinson, private secretary to the governor, and Lieutenant Holt, of the Swedish navy, and fifteen servants were killed. Mr. J. P. Bourke, storekeeper, was wounded, but saved himself by flight. The enemy, I am told, were sixty-two persons, the greater part of whom were the contracted servants and clerks of the Northwest company. They had one man killed, and one wounded. The chiefs, who headed the party of our enemy, were Messrs. Grant and Fraser, Antoine Hoole and Bourrassa; the two former clerks and the two latter interpreters, in the service of the Northwest company."

The above declaration and the following are published in a book entitled "Statement respecting the Earl of Selkirk's settlement, etc.," written by Selkirk's relative, a Mr. Halkett, a director of the Hudson's Bay Co. committee, and it is from this source that most historians have drawn their information relating to the Selkirk side of the case.

The man named Boucher, mentioned by Pritchard in his affidavit, was taken as a prisoner to Montreal, and while there made the following declaration, on the 29th Aug., 1816, before a justice of the peace:

"'Voluntary declaration of Francois Firmin Boucher, accused on oath of having, on the 19th of last June, killed at the colony of the Red River, twenty-one men, among whom was Gov. Semple, says: 'That he did not kill any person whatever; that he was sent, four days before the death of Governor Semple, by one of the partners of the Northwest Company, Mr. Alexander McDonell, from Portage la Prairie, to carry provisions to Frog Plain, about three leagues lower than the fort at the Forks of Red River. That he and his companions, to avoid being seen by the Hudson's Bay settlers, passed at a distance from the Hudson's Bay fort. That, with a view of weakening the Hudson's Bay party, the Bois-Brutes wanted to carry away some of the Hudson's Bay settlers—and, assisted by the deponent to interpret for them in English, they went and carried one off. That, as they proceeded towards Frog Plain, they observed a group of Hudson's Bay people—upon which a certain number of the men in the service of the Northwest Company, called Bois-Brules, joined the deponent and his companions. That these, thinking the Hudson's Bay people meant them harm, (because they advanced with their muskets in their hands) the Bois-Brules wanted to fire on them; but the deponent opposed their doing so. That at last he advanced alone to the Hudson's Bay party to speak to them, and came so near Governor Semple, that the latter took hold of the butt end of the deponent's gun, and ordered his people to advance; that they, not obeying him, and the deponent saying that if they fired they were all dead men. Governor Semple said that they must not be afraid, that this was not a time for it, and that they must fire. Immediately the deponent heard the reports of two muskets fired by the Hudson's Bay people. That at this moments the deponent threw himself from his horse, still holding the mane, and that the horse being afraid, dragged him in this manner about the distance of a gun shot, where he remained. That, from the moment when he was thus carried away by his horse, the firing became general between the people of the Northwest and the Hudson's Bay. That the fire was begun by those of the Hudson's Bay. That the men in the service of the Northwest Company were about sixty-four in number (of whom thirty were at the beginning of the firing,) assembled for the purpose of taking the Hudson's Bay fort by famine. He is not certain, by whose orders, but supposes it was by the chiefs, that is, Mr. McDonell, Mr. Grant, Antonie Oulle and Michael Bourassa. That he heard Mr. McDonell enjoin them to avoid a meeting with the

Hudson's Bay people. That after the firing was over he saw a Bois-Brule named Vasseur near Governor Semple, then wounded in the knee and the arm, who was taking care of him, and who, notwithstanding, had taken his belt or sash, his pistols and his watch, and afterwards carried them away. That he himself had at the moment saved one Pritchard from being killed, and also Francois Deschamps and several other Brules wanted to kill him."

Many of the settlers are of the opinion that the first shot fired was by Lieut. Holt, whose gun went off by accident, thus precipitating the conflict.

In all 21 persons were killed, the remaining eight escaping into the woods, which at that time extended from the highway to the river bank, and making their way to Fort Douglas, one or two swimming the Red River and passing up the east side until opposite the fort. It is to be noticed that only one actual settler was killed.

At the fort all was confusion, the settlers —men, women and children—crowding into the houses within its walls. Mr. Bourke managed to regain the fort with the cannon and a small remnant of the men he took out, and the tale they told struck terror into the hearts of all, who expected an attack would be made immediately by the Northwesters. An anxious night was passed, but no attack came, the Bois Brules having a wholesome dread of the cannon possessed by the colonists.

John Pritchard had been taken as a prisoner to the camp ground of the main body of the Metis, which was situated where the Kildonan ferry landing now is, I am informed by Mr. Donald Murray, whose parents had also been taken prisoners on their farm, two lots above that point, on the morning of the tragedy. He begged of Cuthbert Grant, the leader, to be allowed to go to Fort Douglas. After obtaining permission from Grant, he met with a refusal from the rest of the party; but after giving a promise to return, and agreeing to bear a message to the fort people that they must leave the next day for Lake Winnipeg, he was allowed to depart. Grant accompanied him as far as Seven Oaks, where the bodies of the killed lay upon the ground, but as it was after nightfall when he passed there, he was spared the sight of the horrible scene.

Arriving at Fort Douglas, he informed the settlers that the Metis demanded that the colonists should depart, and had promised that if all public property was given up to them, they would give a safe escort to the people and allow them to take all their personal effects. Two other parties of Northwesters were daily expected to arrive in the Red River, one coming from the Saskatchewan and the other from Lake Superior, and it would be necessary to send some of the

Bois-Brules with them to explain the position of affairs.

The colonists at first refused to agree to the terms of capitulation, and Sheriff McDonell, who was in charge of the settlement, decided to hold to the fort as long as the men were inclined to protect it. In the morning, however, after they had more fully considered their situation, the settlers concluded to depart, and after several visits of the sheriff to the Metis camp an arrangement was agreed on.

HOW THE INDIANS ACTED.

A number of Indians under Peguis were camped on the east side of the river and took no part in the troubles, but their sympathies were plainly with the colonists. They went out the morning after the engagement and brought in the bodies of the killed, or as many as could then be found, for a small number, I am informed by eye-witnesses, were concealed in the heavy brush in the vicinity, as wounded men had crawled into thickets and there died. Mrs. Kaufman, who yet lives in Kildonan east, informs me that she saw the Indians bring in the dead bodies to Fort Douglas with carts, and that Governor Semple and the doctor were buried in board coffins, and the others wrapped up in blankets, the whole number being interred in one large grave in a grove of trees on the south side of the creek southwest of the fort, and quite near the spot whereon now stands the residence of ex-Mayor Logan. She says the body of one man was naked, the clothes having been stolen before the Indians found it. Mr. Donald Murray also informs me that when the burial took place, Chief Peguis stood near by, with the tears streaming down his face, and he repeatedly expressed his great sorrow at the sad occurrences taking place. Donald Murray states positively that all these bodies were removed, some years after, to St. John's church graveyard, but he is not now able to locate the site of their reinterment. He remembers distinctly that on the morning the settlers handed over the fort to the metis, all the ammunition for the cannon was carried down to the river and thrown into the water from the end of a boat moored in the stream.

FORT DOUGLAS CAPITULATES AND THE COLONISTS DEPART.

An inventory of the Hudson's Bay Co.'s property being taken, Cuthbert Grant gave a receipt on each page, worded as follows: "Received on account of the Northwest company by me, Cuthbert Grant, clerk for the Northwest company, acting for the N. W. company."

In two days all was ready, and the colonists, to the number of nearly two hundred, embarked in their boats and once more started for Jackfish House, at the north end of Lake Winnipeg. It would appear that more or less plundering of the effects of the settlers took place before their departure.

On reaching the neighborhood of Netley Creek, the exiles and their escort of Metis met about one hundred Northwesters, under the command of A. N. McLeod, a partner of the Northwest Company, who had just arrived in a number of canoes from Ft. William to assist Duncan Cameron and Alexander McDonel, the evident intention being to retaliate for the taking of the Northwest forts during the previous winter, and to evict the colonists and destroy the settlement. McLeod was a justice of the peace for the Indian territories and 'had also been gazetted a major in the British army in 1814, when commanding a corps of voyageurs raised by the Northwest Company during the American war. He issued warrants and subpœnas for Pritchard, Bourke and three others, all of whom were taken down to Fort William. Gunn is authority for the statement that the Northwest partners spoke kindly to the colonists and urged them to go to Canada, offering them a free passage, but the majority of the disheartened settlers had resolved to return to Scotland and overruled the desire of a minority to accept the proposition of the Northwesters. After a short detention at Netley creek the colonists re-embarked and proceeded on to Jackfish river (Norway House), where they arrived safely, remaining there until the winter, when, after Lord Selkirk's successes at Fort William in 1816 and the capture of Fort Douglas by his people in the spring of 1817, they returned once more to the Red river.

Leaving the posts on the Red and Assiniboine rivers in the hands of their people the partners of the Northwest Company started on their return to Fort William, and on their way down the Red river met the partners and brigades from the north. These people had reached La Bas de la Riviere (Fort Alexander) only to find that no provisions had arrived from Pembina or Brandon House, and they at once started for the Red river to discover the cause.

Lord Selkirk had not been idle this spring, and at an even date with the destruction of the colony, was taking active steps, in Canada, to reinforce his people in the Red River country, but his movements must be described at length.

LORD SELKIRK CAPTURES FORT WILLIAM.

In the autumn of 1815 Lord Selkirk and his family arrived in Montreal, where he was placed in full possession of information concerning the dispersion of his colonists at Red River during the previous summer, when Duncan Cameron had induced 160 of them to accept a free passage to Canada and driven the remaining 40 to Jackfish River. After bringing the matter before Sir Gordon Drummond, the governor of Lower Canada, and urging him to interfere with the North-

westers without any more success than the English partners of the Northwest Co. had met with from the British government when they had petitioned against the action of Lord Selkirk in the Red River country, his lordship proceeded to raise a force of men, trained to arms, which he intended to convey to Assiniboia. At this time several regiments of mercenaries, which had been recruited in Germany and other continental countries, were being disbanded in Canada, the American war being closed, and there taking place a large reduction in the number of troops serving in Canada. Lord Selkirk enlisted in his own service at Montreal 4 officers and 80 men of the De Meuron regiment, and at Kingston 20 men of the Watteville regiment. These men, fully armed and clothed in the uniforms of the British army, were reinforced by more than an equal number of voyageurs.

Lord Selkirk was appointed a justice of the peace both for Upper Canada and the Indian Territories, and a bodyguard of a sergeant and some soldiers of the 37th Regiment was allowed him by the Governor after a statement that he expected an attempt would be made to assassinate him. That doubts were entertained by the authorities as to the use his lordship intended to make of this detachment may be learned by an examination of the orders given to the soldiers, one part of which reads as follows: "You are particularly ordered not to engage yourself, or the party under your command, in any dispute which may occur between the Earl of Selkirk, his engagees and employees, and those of the Northwest company, or to take any part or share in any affray which may arise out of such disputes. By such interference on your part you would not only be disobeying your instructions, but acting in direct opposition to the wishes and instructions of the government, to the countenance, support and protection of which each party has an equal claim. The Earl of Selkirk has engaged to furnish the party under your command with provisions during the time of your absence. You are on no occasion to separate from your party, but to return with his lordship, and on no account to suffer yourself or any of your detachment to be left at any settlement or post in the Indian country."

All being in readiness, this formidable body started via Toronto, Lake Simcoe and Georgian bay for the Red River settlement some time in June, 1816.

A month before this date Miles Macdonnell, the ex-governor of Assiniboia, who had, as a prisoner, been sent down to Montreal by the Northwest partners in the summer of 1815, had preceded Lord Selkirk, with several canoes belonging to the Hudson's Bay Company, and pushed through to the interior, arriving at Lake Winnipeg shortly after the Semple tragedy.

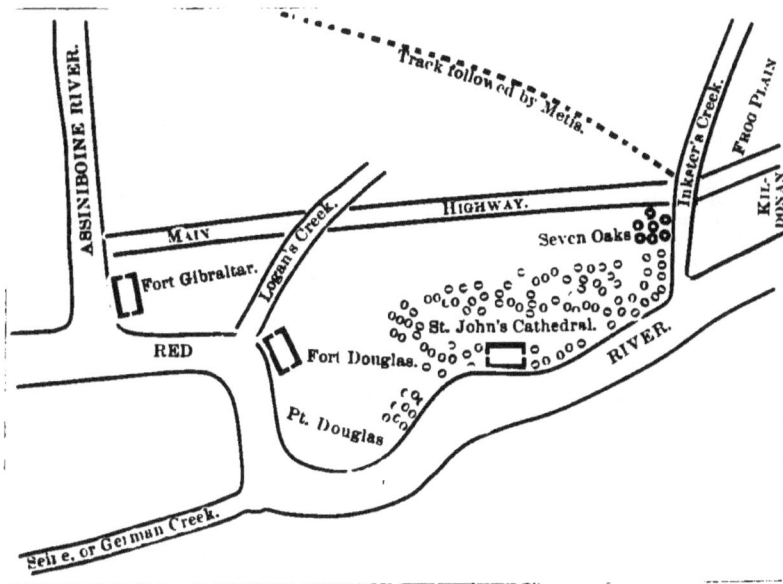

SCENE OF THE SEVEN OAKS FIGHT.

[AUTOGRAPHS from Original Documents Now in Mr. Bell's Possession.]

He immediately returned to Lake Superior, and in the latter part of July met Lord Selkirk with his force near Sault Ste. Marie. His Lordship at once decided to push on to Fort William, the stated original intention having been to reach Assiniboia via Fond du Lac (Duluth,) Red Lake and down the Red River, a route frequently followed by the Northwesters in the early days of the fur trade, but this would have been impossible with the boats passed by Lord Selkirk, and it is most probable that he had always intended to seize Fort William, and the present position of affairs afforded an excellent pretext.

Before leaving Sault Ste. Marie his lordship wrote Sir John Sherbrooke that he intended to interfere as a justice of the peace, and arrest the perpetrators of the outrage. If he had heard of the action of his own people in the Red River country during the preceding spring, when they destroyed the forts of the Northwesters, seized their persons and provisions, and erected batteries of cannon on the banks of the rivers to prevent the passage of their boats, he carefully omits any mention of them in his communications to the Canadian authorities.

The Northwesters at Fort William, in the early spring, had received intelligence of the seizure of their provisions and destruction of forts Gibraltar and Pembina, and A. N. McLeod was despatched with about 60 men in light canoes to protect their interests in that quarter and carry in provisions to supply the brigades from the north. As before related, this party arrived immediately after the killing of Semple and his men. McLeod evidently sympathized with Cuthbert Grant in the way he had managed affairs, for he made presents to the Metis who had been engaged in the fight.

On the 12th August (1816) Lord Selkirk arrived at the Kaministiquia and passing up the river he encamped on the east side half a mile above Fort William.

The Northwesters were busily engaged in making ready for the interior the outfits of goods intended for the winter's trade. The Northwesters claim to have had fully 500 men collected there at that date, the post being the great meeting point where the brigades arriving from Montreal landed their merchandise and received in return the bales of furs brought down from the interior posts, which were strung along in lines reaching to the Pacific. Fort William itself consisted of a score of well constructed houses used as officers', clerks', and men's quarters, messrooms, stores, powder magazine, workshops, etc., etc., the whole being surrounded by a palisade fully 15 ft. in height with a watch tower over the gate. It was built in 1803, when the company moved their headquarters from Grand Portage, which place was in the United States south of the international boundary. It was named after William McGillivray, a chief partner of the Northwest Company.

Lord Selkirk had no sooner encamped than cannon were landed and pointed at Fort William, while a demand was made on Wm. McGillivray, who was in charge, for the release of John Pritchard and others of the Hudson's Bay Co.'s people then in the fort. These were immediately allowed to depart, McGillivray stating that he did not hold them as prisoners, but that two other persons whom he had arrested were on their way to Montreal for trial.

From Pritchard, Nolin and others of his rescued people his lordship procured the details of the events which happened at the settlement, and he issued a warrant for the arrest of Wm. McGillivray.

SELKIRK ARRESTS THE NORTHWEST PARTNERS.

This warrant was served the next day on Mr. McGillivray in the fort, and without hesitation he went over to the Selkirk camp, accompanied by K. McKenzie, another partner, and Donald McLaughlin, the party being received at the Fort William landing by a guard of 20 soldiers, and on their arrival at the Selkirk landing they were met by the soldiers of the 37th Regiment under arms, who conducted them to Lord Selkirk. When one remembers the instructions given to the men of the 37th Regiment, it seems that this was a very irregular proceeding; but Selkirk's object clearly was to impress on the Northwesters the idea that he was acting with the assent of the Canadian Governor.

McGillivray's friends offered bail, but were informed that they also were prisoners charged, like all the partners of the Northwest Company present at the annual meeting of 1814, with being responsible for the troubles at Red River. Warrants were issued for the arrest of other Northwest officials, the mode of executing which are best described by two officers of the De Meuron regiment, who had left Montreal in May on leave of absence with McLeod and other partners of the Northwest Company, to witness the occurrences that would follow Lord Selkirk's advent with his armed force, so that the authorities would receive an impartial account from disinterested persons.

AN ACCOUNT BY WITNESSES.

"Charles Brumby, lieutenant in His Majesty's Regiment de Meuron, and John Theodore Misani, also lieutenant in the same regiment, respectfully depose and say: That in the beginning of May last, they left Montreal, in company with Messrs. Alexander McKenzie, Archibald Norman McLeod, and Robert Henry, on a journey to the Indian Territories in North America, that being arrived at the distance of about fifty miles from the forks of the Red river, in the Indian Territories, on the 23rd of June last, in the morning, they met a number of persons coming from that place, among whom were several of the colonists of the settlement of Lord Selkirk, who informed them that a battle had been fought between the colonists and the half-breed Indians, at the distance of a mile and a half below the fort on the place of residence of Robert Semple, Esquire, agent of the Hudson's Bay Company (called by them, Governor Semple), at the forks of the Red river, and they understood this battle was fought on the 19th of the said month; that the deponents proceeded until they reached the place where they understood that the said Robert Semple had a post or establishment, and there saw a number of Indians (called half-breeds) and other Indians assembled there; and that the deponents remained there but a few hours, and returned to Riviere aux Morts (Netley Creek. Ed.), situated at the distance of about 54 miles from the said forks of the Red River, on their way back to Fort William, that on their arrival at Riviere aux Morts they saw John McDonald, who was arriving from his wintering grounds, and also Simon Frazer, who arrived in canoes; that these two persons could not have been coming from Red River, if they had come by water from that quarter; and that the said John McDonald gave these deponents directions to take some of his provisions on their return to Fort William, at a place he pointed out to them; that they also met at the same place John McLaughlin, whom they had left at Fort William when they passed it; that they met John McGillivray in Lake Minipic (Winnipeg. Ed.) on the 27th day of the said month, as they were going to Fort William, coming, as it appeared to these deponents, and as he informed them, from his wintering quarters that the several persons above - named appeared to be entirely ignorant of what had taken place at the forks of the Red River on the 19th of June, and these deponents verily believe that they were not, and could not have been at that place at the time; that these deponents were informed that the persons concerned in the Northwest trade generally received their provisions at a place called La bas de la Riviere, that is, the entry of the River Winipic, and that the reason of several of them going up the river as far as the Riviere aux Morts was their disappointment in not receiving their provisions at the usual place; that when these deponents left Montreal, on the 1st or 2nd of May last, they saw Mr. William McGillivray at that place, and they found him at Fort William on their return from Red river, where they arrived on the 10th of July last; that on the 13th day of August the deponents, being at Fort William, saw two of the boats that had come the preceding day with a party of men under the Earl of Selkirk; that these two boats were full of soldiers; that D'Orsonnens was in the first boat and Lieut. Fauche

in the second; that on their landing near the gate of the fort a person of the name of McNabb and another person of the name of Allen, both of whom had come in the said boats, approached the gate of the fort with Capt. D'Orsonnens, who was armed with a sword and pistol, and there spoke to several of the partners of the Northwest Company, who stood at the gate; that some words passed between them, and these deponents heard some of the Northwest Company say: "Yes, but we cannot admit so many people in the fort at once." That one-half of the gate was then shut partly. That immediately on uttering the above mentioned words Capt. D'Orsonnens called to the men in the boats, "en evant, aux armes, vites!" upon which the men in the boats jumped out, and, with muskets and fixed bayonets, rushed into the fort, a bugle at the same time sounding the advance; that a number of the men (voyageurs) in the service of the Northwest Co., who stood near the gate, ran towards their encampment; that these deponents observed several of the soldiers dragging Mr. John McDonald towards the boats, swearing at him, and using violence, and heard him cry out, "don't murder me." That these deponents entered the fort, where they saw Mr. Allen, and asked him the cause of such proceedings, who answered that all would be soon explained, and that the person who had ordered these measures would answer for the consequences, or words to that effect; that a few minutes afterwards, Capt. Matthey arrived with a reinforcement of soldiers, which the deponents conceived to have been called for by the sound of the bugle; that there were two pieces of cannon in the fort, which the soldiers planted in the square, and pointed at the gate, and this armed party was immediately in possession of the fort, as no resistance whatever was offered them; that the deponents did not see any of the persons in the fort armed at the time it was so taken possession of by the said armed party; that on the same day the partners of the Northwest Company who were in the fort, nine in number, were arrested, and the deponents saw several of them conducted as prisoners out of the fort with a guard, and they returned about eight o'clock in the evening, and the next day they were put in close confinement, with sentries over them; that on the evening of the 13th the troops marched out of the fort, after having been assembled in the square by the sound of the bugle, with the exception of 20 men under the command of Lieutenant W. Graffenreid, who remained in the fort as a guard for the night; that sentries were posted in several places, and the place had the appearance of a military post; that the next morning Captain Matthey returned to the fort with a number of armed soldiers, and told Mr. Wm. McGillivray on his arrival that he had brought a reinforcement, as they understood that the gentlemen who had been arrested the preceding day, instead of confining themselves to their own rooms, had been going about, and that arms had been preparing, or words to that effect; that a short time after the Earl of Selkirk appeared to take command ; and some days after, he took his quarters in a house formerly occupied by the gentlemen of the Northwest Co., and some of his people were also quartered in other apartments and buildings within the fort. That the deponents also understood that on the following days the books and papers of the Northwest Co. had been seized and searched, and saw at one time, Mr. Allen, Mr. McNabb, Mr. McPherson and Capt. D'Orsonnens, searching for papers and sealing up trunks in different rooms. The deponents also saw some of the soldiers employed in making gun carriages in a workshop, formerly used by the carpenters and men of the Northwest Co. That on the 22nd of August a canoe arrived from Montreal with dispatches, that the papers or despatches the men brought were taken away from them, and the canoe searched; that some of the things in it were placed in charge of a soldier of the 37th regiment, one of the bodyguard of the said Earl of Selkirk; that it appears to these deponents, that from the taking of the fort, as above mentioned, until the time the deponents left it, the trade and business of the Northwest Co. was entirely stopped: that the deponents understood the Northwest Co. were not allowed to send any goods or furs out of the fort, nor could they employ the men in their service, some of whome were destined to go into the interior of the country with goods and ammunition for the natives, and to supply their different trading posts; others to go down to Montreal with furs and other articles for exportation, as the deponents understood."

(Signed) CHARLES BRUMBY, Lieut.
THEODORE MISANI, Lieut.

Sworn at Montreal the 16th of Sept., 1810.

Lieut. Fauche, one of Selkirk's DeMeuron officers who returned from Ft. William, and which came under his notice, entirely agrees with that given above.

THE NORTHWESTERS PROTEST.

The partners of the Northwest company being confined as prisoners, signed a solemn protest to the acts committed by Selkirk and his armed associates, the persons signing being Wm. McGillivray, Kenneth Mackenzie, John Macdonell, John McLaughlin, Hugh McGillis, and Daniel Mackenzie. It is needless to say that no attention was paid to this protest. Lord Selkirk took possession of all the stores and merchandise of the Northwest company as a means to destroy their business which he now had the means of doing, the chiefs of the company being in his

hands. No outfits were allowed to be taken into the interior. Two clerks were nominated by the Northwest partners to look after their interests; but Selkirk gave them no satisfaction, and finally refused to confer with them. One of these clerks, named Vandersluys, afterwards made affidavits of what transpired, and I am informed by an old settler that some years after he came into collision with Mr. Halkett, brother-in-law of Selkirk, who wounded him with a pistol in Montreal.

Lord Selkirk's friends have written a great deal in attempting to prove that he was most careful in keeping within the law in all his proceedings, but no explanation is given of the use he made of the soldiers of the 37th Regiment who had received such strict orders to remain neutral at all times and in all situations.

NORTHWESTERS SENT AS PRISONERS TO MONTREAL.

On the 18th of August Lord Selkirk placed the prisoners in charge of Lieut. Fauche and shipped them off to Canada. Unfortunately, when nearing Sault Ste. Marie, one of their boats was swamped in a squall, and nine persons, out of the twenty-one it contained, were drowned, K. McKenzie being one of the lost. Arriving at York (Toronto), the Governor directed that the prisoners should be taken to Kingston, where the Attorney-General and judges were then on circuit. At Kingston the judges directed them to be taken to Montreal, and on arriving there they were all released on bail. The crimes charged against them were no less than high treason, conspiracy and murder.

Lord Selkirk, after the departure of the partners, fitted out canoes belonging to the Northwesters with property found in the fort, and having seduced some employes and coerced others, sent them inland to the Hudson's Bay Company's posts.

WARRANTS ISSUED FOR ARREST OF SELKIRK.

Wm. McGillivray, after his release on bail, secured warrants for the arrest of Selkirk, Capt. Matthey, and some others, for their high-handed acts in seizing the Northwest Company's property in Upper Canada (Fort William being within Canada and far east of the Indian territories.) A deputy-sheriff with a posse was sent up to Fort William, and arrested Selkirk and the other persons named in the warrants, but they called in the ever-ready De Meurons, who, with fixed bayonets, turned the tables by making the law officers prisoners, and afterwards ejected them from the fort. Selkirk refused to recognize the warrants, and went on seizing all the establishments of the Northwesters about Lake Superior, and went so far as to take possession of the goods and furs stored in the post at Fond du Lac (Duluth), which being on American soil, had paid the U. S. customs duties.

Here, also, prisoners were made and taken to Fort William.

SEIZURE OF RAINY LAKE POST.

One party of Selkirk's men, under command of Fidler went inland to Rainy Lake to the Northwest Co.'s post there (now Fort Francis) and demanded its surrender, but Dease, who was in charge, drove them off. Selkirk then sent an officer and band of De Meurons with two cannon to invest the place, the officer informing Dease that if he did not surrender he could not be answerable for the conduct of his soldiers. Running short of provisions Dease had to capitulate and his post was turned into an establishment of Lord Selkirk, who removed some of the buildings across the river to the U. S. side, apparently not feeling safe on the Canadian side, which was the territory of Upper Canada. This fort was the key to the whole Northwest Territories and its possession fully deprived the Northwesters of any chance of carrying on their trade from Lake Superior.

This state of affairs continued during the winter. Lord Selkirk remained about Lake Superior, the Northwesters held Fort Douglas and the Red river posts, and the Selkirk colonists wintered at Jack Fish River at the north end of Lake Winnipeg, but in the early spring a general activity was manifested by all parties.

THE DE MEURON'S ADVANCE.

In February (1817) Lord Selkirk, from his headquarters in the Northwest company's Fort William, despatched Capt. D'Orsonnens with a large band of his soldiers fully armed and equipped, to the Red River, the expedition going by way of the Rainy River, Lake of the Woods, and from the Northwest Angle striking across the country by land in the direction of what is now known as the Dawson road, but arriving at a point on the Red River some distance south of the entrance of the Assiniboine. Following down the Red River the party diverged to the west and came to the Assiniboine in the neighborhood of St. James' parish, where they made scaling ladders and prepared to assault Fort Douglas, then occupied by the Northwesters. Taking advantage of a wild stormy night, the leader, guided by friendly Indians and whites, marched to the fort and quietly placing the ladders in position scaled the walls and quickly overpowered the occupants. All the principal inhabitants were made prisoners and the others were turned out to shift for themselves, which they did by going to the tents of their friends, the freemen, living along the banks of the Red and Assiniboine rivers.

The fort taken, news was dispatched in all directions, and the exiled colonists at Jackfish river were informed that they might return to their homesteads, when they would be protected by the DeMeuron soldiers. A few colonists started at once on snowshoes for Fort Douglas, and arrived before the warm spring sun broke up the ice on the rivers and lakes, but it was not until June that the main party of colonists arrived on the site of their former homes, when they were joined by Lord Selkirk and his men from Fort William.

TIMES OF SCARCITY.

To find food for such a large number of people taxed the energetic Selkirk, and the river was largely drawn on for the fish it contained, and from all accounts the poor colonists had a very hard time of it until the small quantity of seed they planted in the spring brought forth a harvest, which this year was an enormous one for the acreage under crop. But the demand exceeded the supply, and in the autumn the settlers were again compelled to leave the settlement and proceed to their old time winter quarters at Pembina, in order to be within reach of the buffalo. During the winter many of them were forced to travel on foot to the Missouri Coteau in search of food, the buffalo having disappeared from the country bordering on the Red River.

AT LAST THE BRITISH GOVERNMENT INTERFERES.

Notwithstanding the frequent appeals made to it in England by the partners of the Northwest Company, and in Canada by Lord Selkirk, the British Government had invariably remained passive, and seemingly declined to interfere between the rival interests, or declare the legality or illegality of the claims of either party. The Northwesters notified the Government that they held the claims of Lord Selkirk as illegal, and would resist to the utmost, by force if necessary, any attempt of his lordship to interfere with their trading operations.

After calmly reviewing the whole circumstances of the proceedings at Red River, one must arrive at the conclusion that neither party can be wholly blamed for the dire results of the actions of the chief officials on either side. Governor Miles Macdonnell, assuredly acting under the instructions of Lord Selkirk, annoyed the Northwesters in their trade, and followed it up by acts of violence to the persons and property of people employed by the Northwest Co. The Northwesters resenting this, retaliated. The crowning act of the whole disturbance, the killing of Gov. Semple and his men, without doubt was the result of chance. The Northwesters were under orders to pass at a distance from Fort Douglas, and were doing so when Semple foolishly went out with a party inferior as to point of numbers, and rashly brought on the conflict. Semple evidently believed he was in the right and that the Northwesters were interlopers in the country, while on the other hand the Northwesters had occupied the country and had spent great sums of money in exploring and opening up the fur countries, reaching to the shores of the Arctic and Pacific, years before the Hudson's Bay Co. attempted to follow them, as the Canadians had followed in the footsteps of the French, who, to certain distances had penetrated forty years before the Hudson's Bay Co. had ventured to establish a single post inland from the shores of the Bay. The Company laid claim by a lately-discovered interpretation of a royal charter a hundred and fifty years old, while the Northwesters held by right of discovery and occupation. At last the Imperial Government were forced to recognize the situation, and on February 6, 1817, at the very date when Selkirk was sending his armed forces from Fort William to Fort Douglas the Governor-General of Canada was instructed in the following terms:

"You will also require under similar penalties the restitution of all forts, buildings or trading stations, with the property which they contain, which may have been seized or taken possession of by either party, to the party who originally established the same, and who were in possession of them previous to the recent disputes between the two companies. You will require also the removal of any blockade or impediment by which any party may have attempted to prevent the free passage of traders or others of His Majesty's subjects or the natives of the country with their merchandise, furs, provisions and other effects, throughout the lakes, rivers, roads and every other usual route or communication heretofore used for the purpose of the fur trade in the interior of North America, and the full and free permission of all persons to pursue their usual and accustomed trade without hindrance or molestation."

COMMISSIONERS ARE SENT TO RED RIVER.

Col. Coltman and Major Fletcher were appointed by the Governor-General of Canada to proceed to the fur countries to see that these instructions were carried out and secure full information regarding the acts of both parties.

On arriving at Fort William in the early summer the Commissioners found that the sheriff, who had been arrested and imprisoned by Lord Selkirk when he attempted to serve a warrant on him, had, on the departure of his Lordship for Red River, secured his release and officially taken possession of the place and returned it to the Northwest Co. This sheriff afterwards sued Selkirk for damages and was awarded £500 damages. Arrived at the Red River they immediately executed their commission by compelling each party to restore to the other the property and forts taken by force during the disturbances. After collecting information and taking depositions from many persons they returned to Canada and made an exhaustive report.

SELKIRK EXTINGUISHES THE INDIAN TITLE.

Before Selkirk left the settlement he held a meeting with his colonists, when he gave as free grants the lands which had been improved by the settlers. He also settled his De Meurons in the neighborhood of Point Douglas, and so disposed them that on an alarm being given they could be assembled for offensive and defensive purposes.

Promises were made to the colonists, some of which were never kept, but whether through the neglect of Lord Selkirk or his inability to carry them out is not very clear. One grievance long held by some of the settlers was the breaking of his promise that a Presbyterian clergyman should be sent out to them. His lordship had never, it appears, taken any steps to extinguish the Indian title to the lands he had acquired from the Hudson's Bay company, and now, chiefly through the influence of Chief Peguis, he managed to collect 'together the head men of several petty bands of Indians, who claimed the lands along the Assiniboine and Red River as their hunting grounds. Though some of these were comparatively new-comers, for their residence was of but a few years' date, their claim to the land was undoubtedly good by right of conquest and occupation. On the 18th of July, 1817, the Indians assembled and conveyed to his lordship "all that tract of land adjacent to Red River and Assiniboine river, beginning at the mouth of the Red river and extending along the same as far as the Great Forks, at the mouth of Red Lake river, and along the Assiniboine river as far as Muskrat river, otherwise called Riviere des Champignons, and extending to the distance of six miles from Fort Douglas on every side, and likewise from Fort Daer, (at Pembina) and also from the Great Forks, and in other parts extending in breadth to the distance of two English statute miles back from the banks of the said rivers, on each side," the consideration being that Selkirk should deliver annually, on the 10th October, to the Saulteau and Cree Indians at The Forks of the Assiniboine and at Portage la Prairie, respectively, one hundred pounds of good tobacco. This deed was signed by five Indians, Lord Selkirk, Miles Macdonnell, Thomas Thomas, James Bird and five others.

This business attended to, his lordship took his departure for Canada via Minnesota and overland.

IN THE CANADIAN COURTS.

Much discussion had taken place in Canada over the troubles in the fur countries during 1816-17, the Montreal papers being the common medium through which writers ventilated their views on the situation. On Selkirk's arrival in Upper Canada from the Red River country in 1817 he found awaiting him four charges, made against him by the partners of the Northwest Company. These were for having stolen eighty-three muskets at Fort William; the forcible taking possession of Fort William in 1816; an assault and false imprisonment of the deputy sheriff; resistance to legal arrest. The magistrates dismissed the first charge and accepted bail for his appearance to answer for the others. Commissioner Coltman had taken bail from Selkirk to appear at Montreal, but the courts there changed the trial to Upper Canada.

In September, 1818, his lordship was tried at Sandwich on a charge of "a conspiracy to ruin the trade of the Northwest Company," on which occasion a disagreement arose between the grand jury and the Attorney-General, John Beverley Robinson, on the latter's claim of a right to attend the grand jury and examine the witnesses. The trial never came off and Selkirk left for England. After his departure a true bill was found at York and verdicts were given against him of £500 for the imprisonment of Deputy-Sheriff Smith, and £1500 for the false arrest and imprisonment of McKenzie, one of the Northwest Co.'s partners, at Fort William. It is probable that the Northwesters brought great influence to bear on the authorities in Canada to prevent the trial of some of their employees, but several of those charged with crimes were actually tried by jury before Chief Justice Powell, at York, in October, 1818, but verdicts of "not guilty" were rendered.

SELKIRK'S DEATH.

On his return to England, in 1818, Lord Selkirk seems to have become broken down in health, and crossed over to the continent in search of rest, and a milder climate than England affords, but he never recovered from the effect of the troubles encountered in America. He died on the 8th April, 1820, at Pau, in the south of France, surrounded by his wife and daughters.

NAVAL OPERATIONS ON LAKE WINNIPEG.

Even after the trials in Canada in 1818, the Northwesters were arrested by force in the fur country. In 1818 William Williams was sent out from England to Red River as an official of the Hudson's Bay Co., wintering that year at Cumberland House, on the Saskatchewan. The next summer he applied his knowledge of naval operations (he had been a sailor) to the fitting out of a small schooner for service on Lake Winnipeg. Arming the vessel with cannon, and manning it with the ever-ready DeMeuron soldiers, left by Selkirk as peaceable tillers of the soil, the new governor proceeded to Grand Portage, at the mouth of the Saskatchewan river, which he took possession of, so as to seize the brigades of the Northwest Co., as they arrived from the interior, en route to Fort William.

Unaware of the surprise that awaited them, the Northwesters arrived at the portage and made preparations to cross over it. The soldiers then made prisoners of five partners of the Northwest Company, besides a large number of the junior officials and voyageurs. The officers were Angus Shaw, J. G. McTavish, J. D. Campbell, Wm. McIntosh and Mr. Frobisher. The first two were sent to England; Campbell was forwarded via Moose Factory and the Ottawa River and Montreal, while Frobisher and some of his men were kept in confinement at York Factory until October, when they managed to escape, and finding an Indian canoe, started for the interior, reaching Lake Winnipeg in safety, but without arms or provisions. They suffered so dreadfully from exposure and hunger that poor Frobisher died in misery in November. The remainder of the party, leaving the body unburied, after a few days' travel, reached a Northwester's fort at Moose Lake.

PROGRESS OF THE SETTLEMENT.

The Northwesters' Fort Gibraltar could not be restored to them by the commissioners, for the simple reason that it had been totally destroyed, in 1816, by Selkirk's men, but after the Governor - General's proclamation was enforced the Northwesters went to work and speedily erected a new fort bearing the old name and occupied it until the coalition of the companies in 1821. At Fort Douglas, and lower down the Red River, the Selkirk colonists began to till the ground and erect new dwellings. Many of the De Meurons crossing the river to take land on its east side.

In 1818, when there was every prospect of a bountiful harvest, the grasshoppers appeared and destroyed the crops, leaving the colonists in a state of despondency, which was not lessened by the arrival of some French families from Lower Canada, accompanied by two priests, as the more persons there would be to feed the greater the difficulty in obtaining provisions. Once again, in the autumn, the people made their way to Pembina, in search of that never-failing resource to them—the buffalo. By this time the colonists were more versed in the manner of chasing the "wild cattle of the plains," and in consequence of the near approach of the animals to Pembina an abundance of food was obtained.

In 1819 the Canadians settled at Pembina, while the colonists returned to the settlement at the Forks, where, though they sowed and planted, they reaped not, for the grasshoppers bred early and soon devoured all the green herbage, so that no alternative offered but to travel up to Pembina, as they had so often done before. Almost in despair they settled for the winter on the banks of the Pembina, but during the ensuing winter they secured plenty of provisions, saving enough to take back a supply of pemican for consumption during the seeding time at the settlement in 1820. But the plague of locusts still was upon them, and during the winters of 1820-21, and 1822-23, they were forced back to Pembina. The last season, however, they saved part of their crops.

COALITION OF THE RIVAL COMPANIES.

In 1821, chiefly through the efforts of Edward Ellice, (afterwards the Rt. Hon.), the Hudson's Bay and Northwest Companies consolidated their interests under the title of the first named, securing from the British government, on 6th December, 1821, certain exclusive privileges or trading rights, in the Indian Territories, which included all the lands to the

tion the route to Canada was abandoned for the transport of goods, all the business of the company being done by way of Hudson's Bay, and so it was, that the Canadians, 40 years after, knew little or nothing of the Red River country or its people. The company practically ruled the Northwest under Sir George Simpson, until his death about 1860—though in 1835 a council was chosen from the people resident in the settlement. He was a man of great tact, and managed admirably the affairs of a colony, composed as it was of English, Scotch, Irish, French, Metis and Indians, with their conflicting interests. He annually made the voyage to Red river from Montreal in a bark canoe propelled by the paddles of a large crew of trained and hardy voyageurs, and on one occasion continued his journey by passing

SIR GEORGE SIMPSON.

north and west of the Hudson's Bay territories in British North America, for a term of 20 years. It may here be said that before the expiration of this period, namely in 1838, this license was superseded by one for a further term of 21 years, dating from 1838. It was when the second license was about to expire, and a renewal was asked for, that the Canadian government pressed a claim for the Hudson's Bay Territories, and contested the legality of the company's charter, sending representatives to England for that purpose, the agitation being kept up from 1857 to 1869, when the transfer took place.

In 1821 the means of both companies were nearly exhausted through competition and extravagance, and both parties welcomed a termination of the strife. After the coali-

over the great prairies of the Northwest and the Rocky Mountains, across Behring's strait, through Russia in Asia and Europe, and on to England, from whence he sailed back to Montreal—the first man to pass around the world north of the equator.

SWISS IMMIGRANTS.

In the autumn of 1821 a party of immigrants from Switzerland arrived at York Factory. They were induced to leave Europe in the hope that they would make quiet, steady and peaceable settlers, but on their arrival in the colony, in the early winter, after a very arduous journey at an inclement season, it was found that most of them were rather of the artizan class than agriculturists. On the flyleaf of a church register kept by the Rev. John West, and now on deposit in the English Church archives, is a memorandum that 171 colonists left Europe for the settlement in 1821, and six children were born on the voyage, leaving a total of 177. Next year eight of these left for Canada or the United States, and fourteen were dead. Nearly all these people left the country four years later.

A NEW GOVERNOR.

From the date of Semple's death in 1816, to 1822, Alexander McDonell was, when circumstances permitted, acting as governor of the colony. In 1822 Captain Bulger entered on the duties of the governor's office, George Simpson (afterwards Sir George) being the governor-in-chief.

structed, occupied Fort Gibraltar, and it will be interesting to notice here that the marriage register of the Rev. John West, under date of April 18, 1822, contains an entry of the solemnization of a marriage, George Simpson attesting as witness, at *Fort Gibraltar*, the next six entries made being of marriages at *Fort Garry*, one of which was witnessed by Simpson, while a star is placed opposite the first entry, drawing attention to a foot note, which reads that Fort Gibraltar is "now named Fort Garry." Without doubt, on that date Simpson changed the name to remove any feeling of resentment still existing amongst the Northwestern element at the occupation of it by the new company.

INTERIOR FORT GARRY, 1875.

In 1822 Mr. Halket, a relative and executor of Lord Selkirk, visited the colony and endeavored to arrange its affairs, but the continual trouble experienced by the settlers made this an almost hopeless task. He, however, managed to ameliorate their condition somewhat by throwing off one-fifth of their debts. An arrangement was made whereby goods were sold at the following advance on invoice cost: First 33⅓ was added, then this value was increased by 58 per cent., to make the retail cost to the consumer.

FORT GARRY'S ORIGIN.

The Hudson's Bay Company, as recon-

Nicholas Garry, a member of the Hudson's Bay Company's Council, visited the country about this date, his name appearing, with that of Simpson, as witness to the marriage of Thomas Isbester with Mary Kennedy at Norway House on the 12th of August, 1821.

BUFFALO WOOL COMPANY.

While Gov. Bulger acted as governor of the colony many schemes were entered into by the settlers, such as the formation of the "Buffalo Wool Company." The wool of the buffalo was to be utilized for domestic purposes and export, while the hides of the animals were to be tanned. It is sufficient to say that it was a failure, the concern winding up, with a loss of over $12,000, in the year 1825.

Even in 1823 but few plows were in use, the hoe being the common implement used in farming operations. Gov. Bulger, representing the Selkirk heirs, met with some opposition from the fur-trading authorities of the Hudson's Bay Co., who prevented the settlers from trading horses, leather and provisions from the freemen, but on a proper representation being sent to England these restrictions were removed, though trading in furs was considered a species of high treason, when indulged in by the colonists.

GOV. PELLY.

Gov. Bulger resigned in 1823 and was succeeded by Capt. R. P. Pelly, the fur interests being watched over by Donald McKenzie.

The company now issued, as a circulatory medium, notes of the value of one pound, five shillings and one shilling. It may be said that silver coins were unknown in the country until troops arrived in 1846.

Soon after Capt. Pelly's advent a large band of cattle was brought into the country and sold to the colonists. An experimental farm was started at Hayfield on the east side of the Red River, about three miles above the entrance of the Assiniboine, but, like the Buffalo Wool company affair, gross mismanagement occurred, and it proved an utter failure after a sinkage of $10,000 was made.

THE FIRST RED RIVER CART.

At this time the famous Red River cart was in common use. I find in an unpublished journal of a fur trader that the first cart ever used on the Red River plains was made in the Northwesters' fort at Pembina in 1801, when the wheel was a solid block of wood, about three feet in diameter.

The next year an improvement was made in the wheels, as announced in the following paragraph I have extracted from the manuscript referred to : "They (the carts) are about four feet high and perfectly straight, the spokes being placed perpendicularly without the least bending outwards, and only four in each wheel; the carts will carry about five pieces (450 pounds), and are drawn by one horse." Little improvement was afterwards made in these primitive carriages, and even to-day an occasional cart, drawn by an ox or a horse, may be seen parading the main business street of the capital of the Canadian Northwest.

Gunn informs us that in 1825 iron was worth four shillings a pound in the settlement, and it cost £4 sterling to get the iron-work of a plow.

THE GREAT FLOOD.

In the spring of 1826 the Red river overflowed its banks, and spread over the country for a great distance. The settlers were compelled to fly in haste to the Little Stony Mountain. Their houses, which were almost invariably erected on the first or lower bank of the Red river, were washed away. The previous winter had been a very severe one, the freemen residing about Pembina losing many of their people by exposure and starvation, notwithstanding the efforts of the colonists to supply them with food, under the direction of Donald McKenzie, the head officer of the Hudson's Bay Co. Now it was the turn of the colonists to suffer, as had often been the case before. Not until the flood reached to sixteen feet over usual high water mark did the raging waters show any sign of abating, and though the torrent first surged over the river banks on the 2nd of May, it was not until the middle of June that the waters receded to below the level of the banks of the stream. Nearly every possession was scattered and ruined, and the wretched people met to consider what course they should pursue. Finally the Scotch and French decided to begin anew the erection of houses, with the intention of remaining in the country, but the DeMeurons and Swiss, almost to the last individual, determined to leave the settlement. On the 23rd June, assisted by the Hudson's Bay company's officials with provisions, 243 persons started for Fort Snelling in the neighborhood of where now stands St. Paul, Minnesota. They arrived in safety at their journey's end, after passing through the lands of the warlike Sioux, and many of their descendants are to-day among the most prominent and prosperous of the Western States.

The colonists who remained set to work with a will, and, while some erected new dwellings, on the highest bank of the Red River, others sowed what little seed had been preserved. The harvest was a generous one, and the following winter was passed by the people in enjoyment of an abundance of provisions.

THE COUNCIL OF ASSINIBOIA.

For some years after matters in the colony were very quiet, the harvests being good and provisions in plenty. It was in 1835 that Sir George Simpson became the president of an executive body known as the government or council of Assiniboia. This council was composed originally of the governor of Rupert's Land, the governor of the Selkirk colony (who was also a chief factor in the Hudson's Bay Co.), the Roman Catholic bishop, two clergymen of the English church, several retired officers of the company, and a few residents of the colony.

MISSIONARIES.

In 1820 the Rev. John West arrived in the settlement from England to serve as chaplain for the Hudson's Bay Company, and immediately visited the company's posts throughout the country, marrying and baptizing the people. The first entry in the baptism register, which is still in existence, is dated September 9, 1820, being that of William, son of Thomas and Phœbe Bunn. He administered the rite of baptism on 239 occasions before the close of 1822, and during that time married 54 couples. The clergyman's fees were, for marriages, 5 shillings; for burials, 2 shillings and 6 pence, and for certificates, 2 shillings and 6 pence. In the autumn of 1823 the Rev. D. Jones replaced Mr. West, with the title of assistant chaplain, but after August 18, 1825, he assumed the title of chaplain. The registers contain entries made by George Harbidge, missionary school-master. In 1825 the Rev. W. Cockran arrived in the settlement, and shortly after settled at the rapids, in St. Andrews parish, Mr. Jones at the time residing at what is now known as St. John's, though it then formed a part of Kildonan. It was not until the 28th of October, 1853,

settlers. Besides an experimental farm, one of these was the growth of flax, but while the plant grew well, and abundant harvests were gathered, the result of the venture was a failure, on account of scarcity of laborers and absence of skilled workmen. The next undertaking was the formation of "The Tallow Company" in 1832. Nearly 500 head of cattle were secured in the settlement and placed under the care of herders who were inexperienced and incompetent, with the result that 111 animals were lost during the first year. Though the investors had been promised great profits from the hide and tallow export trade, none appeared, and the company was broken up in 1834.

In 1833 a joint stock herding company was formed with a capital of £1,200. Two men were sent to Missouris for sheep to start a ranche, but owing to personal disagreement between them they pushed on to Kentucky to make their purchase. Some

FIRST ANGLICAN CHURCH.

that St. John's church was consecrated by that name. From 1821 to 1830 a large number of retired officials and servants of the company became residents of the settlement, most of them taking up land north of Fort Garry along the Red river. Owing to the attitude of the French Metis to the Hudson's Bay Company, Governor Simpson in 1831-34 erected, in the heart of the English settlement, the establishment ever since known as the Lower or Stone Fort.

A SPECULATION MANIA PREVAILS.

The Selkirk settlers were greatly in debt to the Selkirk heirs, and as the market for farm produce was extremely limited, they were unable to pay off the existing indebtedness. Several schemes were entered into in the hope that the export of farm produce would increase the direct revenue of the

1,475 sheep were purchased at from five to seven shillings each, and the drove started for Red River. Overdriven and illused by the carelessness of those in charge only 251 were surviving at the end of the journey.

Having gone through this experience of sheep raising, something else must be undertaken, so, in 1837 Captain Cary was brought out from England by the H. B. Company with a full staff of servants, and outfits of the most improved farming implements. The buildings of old Fort Garry were utilized as farm houses and barns, the farm itself being situated on the lands adjoining, or what are to-day known as the Hudson's Bay Flats. From 1837 to 1847 the farm flourished to a small extent, but old settlers inform me that the employees engaged there ate the bulk of the produce raised, and that the

costly experiment ended in the breaking up
of the farm, after great loss to the Hudson's
Bay Company.

Some time before, during the existence of
the experimental mania, the Company im-
ported from England, via Hudson Bay, the
celebrated stallion Fireaway, whose descendants are still highly prized by the Red
River people.

In 1835 the Hudson's Bay Company purchased from the Selkirk heirs all their rights
in the colony, with the lands included in
the grant made to Lord Selkirk in 1811,
the price paid being variously stated at
from £36,000 to £86,000.

LAW MAKING.

In the same year (1835) the council of Assiniboia was called together, when Sir Geo.
Simpson explained that the time had arrived when it was necessary make laws for the
government of the population, which had
risen to about 5,000 souls. Accordingly,
the territory was divided into four districts,
in each of which quarterly courts, presided
over by a magistrate, were established.
These courts had power to pronounce final
judgments in civil cases where the debt
or damage claimed did not exceed five
pounds. Appeals might be allowed at the
discretion of the magistrate to a supreme
court, which was the council of Assiniboia itself. In cases involving
claims of more than ten pounds, and in
all criminal cases, a jury was to decide
by its verdict the facts in dispute.

The council also levied an import duty of
seven and one-half per cent. on all goods
brought into the country, and while guard-
ing the fur-trading interests, they also
placed an export duty on provisions and live
stock, the growth or produce of the colony.
A gaol was constructed immediately after
the passing of these laws, the sum of £300
having been given as a gift to the colony by
the fur-trading branch of the Hudson's Bay
Co.

On the 28th April, 1836, the first trial by
jury took place, when one Louis St. Dennis
was convicted of theft and sentenced to be
flogged in public. The sentence was at once
carried into effect, to the indignation of the
assembled crowd, who expressed their feeling by throwing stones at the flogger.

TRADE WITH THE UNITED STATES.

About this date the Red River people
were beginning to open up a traffic with
the American settlements on the Missis-
ippi, and several men had established stores
on their own account. Andrew McDermot
and Robert Logan, who names are borne by
estates and street in the city of Winnipeg
of to-day, were among the most prominent.
Trading in furs was, however, strictly prohibited. The French were, as a rule, the
hunters of the country, gathering in great
camps for the purpose of proceeding to the
buffalo country, situated towards the Missouri
river. The camps were regulated by certain

unwritten laws, called for by the necessities
of the situation. Chiefs were elected who
sternly enforced the rules agreed to by all
who enjoyed the protection afforded by the
presence, in the Sioux country, of a semi-
military force. Cuthbert Grant, the old
Northwester, was denominated the
"Warden of the plains." Many an en-
counter took place between the Metis and
the Indians, but almost invariably the
latter were beaten with great loss, and they
finally sued for peace with the mixed
bloods. Much trouble arose at times between the Company and the Metis on
account of the fur trading proclivities of
the latter.

The English and Scotch settlers, while
perhaps indulging to a limited extent in
buffalo hunting, were the agriculturists of
the colony and bowed to the dictum of the
legal authorities more readily than their
French neighbors and friends.

In 1839 Adam Thom appeared in the
settlement as recorder of Rupert's Land.
He acted as a judge in the colony and was
paid by the company until the year 1854,
when he departed.

THOMAS SIMPSON, THE ARCTIC EXPLORER.

The next year Thomas Simpson, who had,
with Mr. Dease, made most valuable explorations from the mouth of the McKenzie
river, eastward along the coastline of the
Arctic ocean, when proceeding across the
plains south of Pembina, en route to England to make his report, was either killed
by his companions or committed suicide,
(the actual facts have never yet been
revealed.) His body was brought
back to the settlement and
some degree of obscurity surrounds
the circumstances attending his burial. It
is claimed that owing to the strong preju-
dices of the Scotch on account of his sup-
posed suicide, the remains were not given
Christian burial. Having searched the
burial register of the St. John's church, I
find therein an entry signed by Wm. Cockran, the resident Anglican clergyman, to
the following effect: "Thomas Simpson,
chief trader, Hudson's Bay Co.'s service.
Oct. 15th, 1841. About 32 years." It was
impossible for the clergyman to have made
the entry without performing the duties of
his office.

AN INDIAN HUNG.

The first execution in Assiniboia took
place on the 5th September, 1845, when a
Saulteau Indian killed a Sioux, who was
visiting Fort Garry, by shooting him, the
bullet, after passing through the Sioux's
body entered that of a Saulteau, who also
fell dead. The murderer was hung from a
scaffold erected over the gaol gate, which
building stood a little to the northwest of
Fort Garry.

BRITISH TROOPS.

Various reasons have been given for the
necessity for the presence of British troops

in Assiniboia. It is likely that the complications arising out of the settlement of the Oregon boundary line induced the British governmen to despatch, via York Factory, the 6th Royal regiment (347 men) under Col. Crofton, in 1846; though it is possible that the insecurity of the Hudson's Bay Co. in their exclusive fur trading privileges caused the company to represent strongly to the government the necessity for the presence of troops. The 6th regiment departed in 1848, and were succeeded by a force of 70 pensioners the same year, a reinforcement coming out the following season. These pensioners were commanded by a Major Caldwell, who also acted as governor.

MONOPOLY IN FURS DISAPPEARS.

In the spring of 1849 a serious disturbance took place on the occasion of the trial of a French half-breed named Wm. Sayre, on the charge of illegally trading for furs with the Indians, contrary to the laws of the land, founded on the terms of the Hud-

KILDONAN CHURCH.

son's Bay Company charter of 1670. On the 17th May, when the trial took place, the Metis gathered in force. They were armed, and plainly avowed their intention of resisting the punishment of the prisoner if he was found guilty of the charge. No violence was offered to any person by the crowd, but the authorities recognized that they would be unable to enforce the decision of the court if it should prove unfavorable to the prisoner, and, although he pleaded guilty, he was allowed to depart, on some quibble of his claim to having received permission from an official to trade. The verdict was received by the waiting crowd as an admission by the company that the monopoly in the fur trade was broken, and with loud cries they fired salutes from their

guns and congratulated themselves on their victory.

AMERICANS PURCHASE INDIAN LANDS.

The Americans extinguished the Indian title to the lands along the upper Red river in 1851, Governor Ramsay, of St. Paul, Minnesota, visiting Pembina for that purpose. Much disappointment was experienced by those settlers of the colony who claimed land on the American side of the boundary on the grounds of squatters' rights when they failed to get their claims recognized.

THE FLOOD OF 1852.

A flood, almost as extensive as that whic ruined the settlers in 1826, was experienced in 1852, the damage ensuing being much greater than on the former occasion, as the colonists possessed more destructible property and the population was vastly larger. Every assistence was rendered to the sufferers by the governor and the bishop of Rupert's Land, the clergy generally doing all in their power to encourage and help the people. The Rev. John Black had arrived

REV. JOHN BLACK.

the previous year to become pastor to the Presbyterians, and he labored faithfully then as he did until his death in 1882.

COURT JUDGES.

In 1854 Mr. Thorn was succeeded as clerk to the court (the position of recorder having been abolished) by Judge Johnson, who held the office until 1858, when Dr. Bunn was installed, attending to the duties until his death in 1861. Governor Wm. Mc-Tavish then filled the position for a year, until John Black took over the office.

POPULAR AGITATIONS.

As the population of the settlement increased, in like ratio did the difficulties of administering the laws. The most of the people became dissatisfied with the form of government existing, which was practically the creation of the Hudson's Bay Company. By the year 1857 a considerable trade was carried on between the colony and the United States, where the people, in their annual trips to St. Paul, had presented to them the evidences of the westward march of civilization and settlement in the Western States of the Union.

PETITIONS TO CANADA.

Petitions were sent in 1857 to the legislative assembly of Canada, praying that the Canadian Government would take steps to open up communication between Upper Canada and the Red River, via Lake Superior, and extend to the settlers the protection of Canadian laws and institutions. The Canadian Assembly took immediate action in the premises, and, as the Hudson's Bay Company were then asking from the Imperial Government an extension of their license for exclusive trading privileges in the Indian territories, they protested the claims of the company and asked that the Red River country be handed over to Canada. Representatives were sent by Canada to England and negotiations were entered into with the Imperial Government. An immense mass of correspondence on this matter has been published by both the Dominion Government and that of Ontario in connection with the settlement of the western boundary of Ontario. It was not until 1869 that an amicable settlement of the question was arrived at.

CANADA TAKES POSSESSION.

The Hudson's Bay and Indian territories became part of Canada and the Hudson's Bay Company received as an equivalent £300,000, and extensive land grants.

Troops were sent to Red River in 1857, the Royal Canadian Rifles furnishing the detachment, which consisted of 120 men. This force left Red River in 1861, via York Factory.

THE FIRST STEAMBOAT.

An event occurred in 1862 which created great excitement in the settlement. A steam boat of the flat-bottomed build, which had been constructed on the Upper Red River made its appearance at Fort Garry, bearing several passengers of note and a goodly assortment of freight. The delight of the settlers was almost unbounded as they viewed the good ship Anson Northup, the first steam-propelled craft to ply the waters of the Red River.

SIOUX MASSACRE IN MINNESOTA.

In 1862 the Sioux Indians in Minnesota, taking advantage of the American civil war, took to the war path and massacred many of the settlers in the State. Great fears were entertained by the Red River settlement people that an attack would be made on them, but the Sioux were too wily to take such a step, and had arranged to retreat across the International

line when hard pressed by the U. S. troops. On the suppression of the uprising large numbers of these Indians crossed into Assiniboia, and on the 4th March, 1864, Major Hatch, the officer commanding the American troops stationed at Pembina formally applied to Mr. Dallas, who was governor of the Red River Settlement, for permission to cross with his soldiers for the purpose of attacking the refugee Sioux on British soil. Gov. Dallas, within twenty-four hours, granted permission, only stipulating that no blood should be shed in the houses or enclosures of the settlers, but Major Hatch never availed himself of the opportunity. Many American writers have fallen into the error of stating that Governor Dallas refused Hatch's request, but the writer has in his possession copies of the correspondence which passed between the gentlemen to the above effect. The truth appears to be that Major Hatch forwarded the correspondence to Washington, and was immediately ordered to refrain from crossing the boundary line. During the Indian troubles, communication between St. Paul and Fort

SENATOR SCHULTZ.

Garry was almost entirely cut off. Dr. Schultz, in a speech delivered in the Canadian House of Commons, described a journey made by him from St. Paul to the settlement, when on encountering bands of the Sioux, the explanation that he was a British subject acted as a certificate for free passage. Many of the Sioux who crossed to the north of the line never returned to the United States, though they have never been recognized by government as other than foreign Indians.

NEW-COMERS ON THE SCENE.

In 1863 a change was made in the affairs of the Hudson's Bay Co., by the sale to a new company of all the property and privileges of the old concern.

Canadians and Americans had arrived in the settlement, principally after 1857, when the surveys and explorations conducted by officials of the Canadian government drew attention to the country. Numerous exploring expeditions had passed through the Northwest en route to the far north from the time Sir John Richardson descended the McKenzie river. Back, Simpson and Dease, Lefroy and others had made more or less extended explorations in the geographical and scientific fields, so that gradually information was reaching the outside world of the land that was soon to be thrown open for settlement under the sheltering care of the Dominion of Canada.

A SHORT-LIVED GOVERNMENT.

In 1867 a provisional government was organized by Mr. Thomas Spence, the territory embraced in the scheme being that portion of the present province of Manitoba situated about Portage la Prairie, but when the originators sent home a petition asking for recognition by the Imperial Government, they were informed that the whole proceeding was illegal, and the scheme fell to the ground. The district mentioned was outside the territory included within the bounds of Assiniboia. No serious attention has ever been paid to this movement, the whole matter being now treated as a huge joke.

DISTRESS IN THE COLONY.

A grasshopper visitation took place in 1868 and the people were much distressed for provisions. A committee was formed and subscriptions poured in from Great Britain, Canada and the United States to pay for the wheat and other provisions despatched overland from Minnesota to Fort Garry. The Canadian government proceeded to construct a road from Fort Garry to the Lake of the Woods as a means to afford relief and employment to the settlers, but trouble occurred between the French Metis and the officials in charge of the work.

A CANADIAN GOVERNOR.

In 1869 the arrangements for a transfer of the Hudson's Bay Territories to Canada were concluded and it was announced that the Hon. William Macdougall had been appointed as the first governor to the province about to be formed by Canada. He proceeded to Pembina with a numerous retinue, having great stores of furniture, firearms, ammunition, etc., and on his arrival there found that many of the residents of the settlement, and especially the French, opposed to his entry, the latter being very much annoyed that surveys were being made by Canadian officials, while the people of the settlement had never been communicated with by either the Imperial or Canadian governments or the Hudson's Bay Company regarding the transfer. Mr.

Macdougall announced himself as governor, and issued proclamations, to which no attention was paid.

THE RIEL GOVERNMENT.

Meetings were held at Fort Garry and elsewhere, guards were placed by the French to prevent Governor Macdougall and his people from coming into the country, and then the French took possession of Fort Garry, Louis Riel acting as their chief. More meetings were held, some of them attended by representatives of the English-speaking people, but the final result was that Louis Riel formed a provisional government and ruled the land until the end of August, 1870, when General Wolseley ousted him from the fort on the arrival of the regulars and volunteers sent from Eastern Canada, via Lake Superior, for that purpose.

It is beyond the scope of this paper to refer in detail to the proceedings of the Riel government, it only being necessary to say that the Selkirk settlers, in all circumstances, remained loyal to the British crown.

After 1870 the tide of emigration turned toward Manitoba, and while the country is gradually becoming dotted over with the new settlers, none of them are more respected than the old Selkirk settlers and their descendants, and none of them have suffered the trials and hardships endured by the pioneers.

SELKIRK SETTLEMENT SURVIVORS.

The writer has come into contact with many of the original settlers who came out with the various parties via York Factory to take up lands on the Red River under the auspices of Lord Selkirk, and has secured much information of a general nature regarding life in the Selkirk settlement in the days of its infancy. During this summer I have personally interviewed the last survivors of the original colony who were old enough on the date of their arrival to remember the events that transpired in connection with the trouble between Lord Selkirk and the Northwest Fur company. Herewith I give the substance of the information obtained from these old people at, in cases, many conversations held with them, and wherever possible I use their own words. In the case of Mr. Murray, who is a wonderfully clear-minded and physically active old gentleman, the information, as regards dates and occurrences given by him, have been compared with original documents in my possession, and with such data as is contained in the official church registers of St. John's church. In every case his memory has been proved to be singularly perfect, even the most minute details of his evidence being borne out by the records. It is then safe to accept his statements where contemporary written records are wanting, and it is particularly

WINNIPEG IN 1870.

noticeable that the other survivors of the first] settlement, whom I have conversed with, have referred me to Mr. Murray as *the one* who is the best authority living. Canon Matheson, of St. John's college, kindly procured for me from his father, Mr. John Matheson, the particulars given by him regarding certain points of history in dispute, or not before recorded, in connection with the history of the settlement.

DONALD MURRAY, OF KILDONAN, MANITOBA.

My name is Donald Murray; I was born at Kildonan, Sutherlandshire, Scotland, in or about the year 1801. I came to this place in 1815, with Lord Selkirk's fourth party of colonists, and I have lived here ever since. I remember perfectly well Lord Selkirk's being here in 1817, but I was then too young to be now able to recall anything in particular about him personally. I employed for many years after Michael Lambert, the bugler of the party of DeMeurous that came up with his lordship. I remember, however, that Lord Selkirk held a great meeting with the colonists close to the spot where the Kildonan ferry now is, by the church lot. This was after we returned from Jack Fish [River, now called Norway House, where we had taken refuge after the destruction of the settlement by the North-west men in 1816. At this meeting new arrangements were made with all the settlers as to their lands. Before leaving Scotland the agreement was that we should pay five shillings an acre for our lands, but at this meeting Lord Selkirk gave them to us free of charge. Some of the arrangements made at this meeting were, however, never carried out. His lordship left us in August, going down

by land through the United States. When Governor Miles Macdonald finally left the colony for Canada, [He was present as late as 1817, when he signed the Indian treaty with Selkirk.—ED.] where he afterwards died, a young settler and I went to him and said, "Now, Governor, you know you have in your possession many papers relating to Lord Selkirk's grants of land and other matters, which are of great value to us colonists. Will you not give them to us before you leave?" "No, Donald," says he, "they were given into my charge, and I must keep them." [The papers referred to are likely those now filed in the Dominion archives office at Ottawa.—ED.]

I remember Governor Semple well. He was a very fine man, one of the best that ever came to the settlement. He was a portly gentleman, rather stout and short. He arrived here in the autumn, and during the winter went west to visit the various posts in the interior, returning in the spring, soon after which he was killed. Whilst at the colony he always lived at Fort Douglas. The Seven Oaks massacre took place near the bridge which is close to where Sheriff Inkster's house stands. The half-breeds were coming on purpose to destroy the settlement and kill the settlers. They had been sent by "White-Headed McDonel," as Alexander McDonel was invariably called. After Lord Selkirk arrived McDonel fled to the States and we never heard of him again. I knew Cuthbert Grant, the leader of the half-breeds at the time of the massacre, well in after years, indeed, he was quite a friend of mine, and after my marriage often came to visit me at my house. He always spoke quite freely of the intention of the half-breeds to destroy the colony. Had he acted according to his intention we should certainly all have been killed, but after the massacre of Semple and his party, he acted very kindly towards us, allowing us to take away all our property, or as much as we conveniently could.

The day after the massacre, the Indian Peguis obtained leave to bring in all the bodies in his carts and bury them, which he did. Governor Semple and 19 others were buried near the fort on Point Douglas, close to where Alexander Logan's house now stands. Peguis was very sorry for the death of Gov. Semple. I myself saw him cry like a child as he lowered the body into the grave. This was certainly the morning of the day after the fight. The statement that the bodies were allowed to lie out on the prairie for a fortnight, and that they were mutilated and partially eaten by the wolves, is false. Between the years 1820 and 1830 the remains of those killed were taken up and removed to St· John's church-yard, but no stone was erected over them and I could not now point out the spot where they were re-interred.

I came out in 1815 with my parents. Two brothers of mine had come out a couple of years before us, but they had been sent down to Canada by the Northwest Co. people before our arrival in the settlement. We had a fine voyage out and no sickness among the people. We left Thurso, as near as I can recollect, early in June, and landed at York Factory, as I clearly remember, on August the 17th. We arrived at the settlement I suppose about the end of October. It was a very cold, snowy fall,and we had a hard and stormy journey up from York.

The morning after the Semple murder my father and mother were taken prisoners by the French, as they were working in their field (now lot 25, Kildonan). They had come down from Fort Douglas that morning to work, having been at the fort for some days on account of the reports cir-culating that the French were coming to attack the settlement. They were living in a house which was one of the two erected by my brothers, who had gone to Canada with the settlers led away by Duncan Cameron. My parents were kept as prisoners until the next day.

I think John Matheson (living at Grass-mere now), George Bannerman, John Polson and myself are the only four males alive now of the original colonists; but I think there are several females yet surviving. One is Mrs. Kaufman, who lives in Kildonan, on the east side of the river. [Adam McBeth, of Qu'Appelle, and his brother, both living yet, were infants when they arrived, but should be mentioned as original settlers, and there may be a few similar cases.—ED.]

Fort Douglas was carried away by the flood of 1826. It stood on the northeast side of the little creek that empties into the Red River near where Mr. Logan's house now stands on Point Douglas, but its site is now a long way out in the river, or at least from the present high bank.

The Northwest Co.'s fort was called Gib-raltar, and stood on the Assiniboine point, at the mouth of that river, but it has now all gone into the river a good many years, I think. I do not know of any traces of any earlier fort, known as Fort Rouge, standing near its site. The Hudson's Bay Co., however, had a fort which stood close to where Notre Dame street east is now. This was the fort which Dr. Bryce was unable to locate when he wrote his book about the old forts. This fort was built by Peter Fidler about 1817-18, but he went to Brandon House in the latter year, and it was first occupied by one James Sutherland, who finished it in 1819. As nearly as I can locate its position, it was situated between what is now McDermott and Notre Dame streets east, but perhaps nearer Notre Dame than the other. It was near the rise in the ground and a few hun-dred yards from the Red river. It was about square, the principal entrance facing exactly to the point between the two rivers.

At the farther end, opposite to this gate, stood the master's house, which was larger than the others, ranged down each side of the pallisaded enclosure, about four on each side, but I do not remember exactly how many there were. There was a walk behind, between them and the pal-isades, and an open court-yard in the centre. I think there was also a small powder magazine behind the master's house. I often slept in this fort, and in 1818, when I went to Brandon House, I

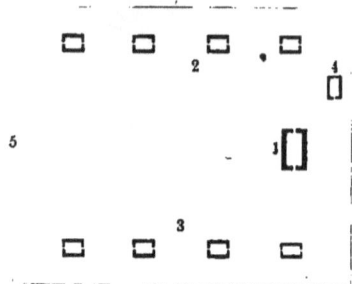

FIDLER'S FORT.

1. Master's House.
2. Houses on southwest side.
3. Houses on northeast side.
4. Powder Magazine.
5. Main Gate, facing Assiniboine Point.

started from it. I do not recollect that it had any particular name other than "the company's fort." It was quite distinct from Fort Garry, and stood at the same time as Forts Douglas and Gibraltar. I forget just when it disappeared, but it probably stood till the flood of 1826, and was then swept away, like the remains of Fort Douglas,then owned by Mr. Logan. If you doubt that this fort was there, just find out about a marriage ceremony I was at in it. I was the only guest from the colony invited when the following persons were married by the Rev. John West: James Bird, the chief factor, to a daughter of Thomas Thomas; Thomas Thomas, a retired chief factor, to Miss Monture; and Joseph Bird, a son of James, to a swampy Cree woman. (Rev. John West's marriage register, now in St. John's Church, shows these entries, and are dated at Red River Colony.--Ed.) I also remem-ber Joseph Bird, a half brother of the late Dr. C. J. Bird, who was speaker in the Manitoba parliament in 1874, built three York boats there in 1819, and those boats, with one made by a boat-builder who was here then and whose name I cannot at this moment call to mind, were taken to York for freight. Just ask old John Matheson if he does not remember that his father worked on that fort for Peter Fidler. I re-member seeing him. [See testimony of Jno. Matheson.—Ed.]

Fort Garry was built by Governor Pelly in 1825, but was washed away the year after by the flood. It was a fine fort, and stood near old Fort Gibraltar. Directly after the flood the Company built houses on the Assiniboine west of Gibraltar, and it was afterwards palisaded. A French Canadian named Basil, or Jacko Laurence, took the contract for the stockade, which was a very fine one.

After the last Fort Garry (part of which yet remains) was built by Governor Christie in 1835-36, the old fort on the point was used as the farm buildings, and some stables were erected by Captain Cary north of them, near where the Broad-way bridge now is, at least they were between the point and that place. (Cellar holes and burnt plaster may be seen to-day at this place.—Ed.) Capt. Cary had the celebrated stallion Fireaway there in charge for the Hudson's Bay Co., and when he left the settlement he took Fireaway with him to the States, having purchased him from the company, much to our sorrow. I freighted to York for Capt. Cary during two or three years after 1844.

Fort Garry for years was only called "The Company's fort" by the settlers, and it was not until the last fort was erected that it was regularly called Fort Garry, though, of course, that was its proper name for years before.

The Hudson's Bay Company used an old building, that stood about 200 or 300 yards north of Fort Gibraltar, as a stable. That was after the companies joined. I do not know if they ever had a fort there before, but they used that old building as a stable when they moved up and occupied the Northwest Company's fort about 1821.

Before we came to the country the Hudson's Bay Company had a store on the east bank of the Red river, opposite to the mouth of the Assiniboine, I think on the property where Mr. N. W. Kittson afterwards had his trading store. The Company may have had a fort there, but I only know for a fact that they had some kind of a store.

The abandoned Hudson's Bay Company's fort at Selkirk in 1815 was on the east side of the Red river, at the end of the big island at the swamp. The chimneys then stood about six feet high. It was called Fort William. There was also a small post four miles south of Netley creek.

In 1818 I saw the company's Brandon House post, which was perhaps a mile or more west of the mouth of Souris river, to which place I walked one day, and it was on the south side of the Assiniboine. The Northwest fort was directly across the Assiniboine from it, on the north side.

The country about the Lower Fort Garry was called the Red Deer plain. [Called the same in Henry's journal of 1800, the St. Andrew's Rapids also being termed the Red Deer Rapids.—Ed.]

When Governor Semple left Fort Douglas to meet the French he had with him only a few men, but the settlers, coming into the fort and hearing of his departure, took their guns and went after him. Some joined him, but others were only half way when the fighting began. Mr. Bourke was on horseback going after the governor, but when he heard the shots he turned back for a cannon, which he took out, and saved some of the people who escaped the massacre. Chief Peguis, who had 70 warriors, shortly before the massacre offered his services to the governor for the defence of the colony, but the governor declined, not thinking there was any danger. The morning after the massacre, before Fort Douglas was given up to the French, we took all the ammunition for the cannoos and threw it into the river, from the end of a boat which was tied to the shore. The cannon balls must now be in the mud at the bottom of the river, quite a long way from the present bank, as the river is much wider now than it was then. An Irishman, named Paddy Clabby, saved a fine sword, which may have been Governor Semple's, by carrying it down from the fort to the river and sinking it in the water, attached to a line, the other end of which was tied to one of the boats we started for Jackfish river in. In this way the sword was towed along unperceived by the French, until it could with safety be taken aboard.

Plenty of muskets came out with the first settlers, but I never heard of them being served out to the colonists. They were stored in Fort Douglas, and one day, in Governor Bulger's time, when I was a constable, I and my companion had them all out in the court yard and cleaned them. I have never heard of the colonists being drilled to arms. Two brass field pieces came out with some of the settlers. One time when Mr. Halket, a relative of Lord Selkirk, and a member of the Hudson's Bay Company's Committee, was out here, he took the wheels of one of the gun carriages, which were of English oak, iron bound, and very strong, to transport his boat to Lake Manitoba, which lay in the route of the trip he was taking. These wheels were left at the mouth of the White Mud River, where they rotted away.

Lord Selkirk was a tall, slender man, probably six feet in height. He had never before been in the Red River country when I saw him in 1817.

I do not remember ever having heard of Lord Selkirk's sending out any reindeer from Norway, but he did send out a herd of Orkney cattle.

I remember Duncan Cameron of the Northwest Company, who was a fine old gentleman, much liked by the people, also his brother Reynold, who died at Pembina. In 1816, Colin Robertson did not agree well with the officials in the settlement. They did not like him, neither did the settlers. As he started off with a boat containing fur for Lake Winnipeg, in derision he hoisted a pemican sack inatead of a British flag as was usual. This was before the Semple affair. After the massacre the Northwesters occupied Fort Douglas, but erected new houses at Fort Gibraltar in 1817-18 after Col. Colt-

was a back gate on the north side by which wood was taken in. The fort stood twenty or thirty yards back from the rivers, which at that time were much narrower than now.

Lord Selkirk gave a free grant of fifty

HUDSON'S BAY COMPANY DOG TRAINS.

man, the commissioner, came here. Fort Gibraltar was positively situated on the very point of land between the rivers, although the main face and principal gateway overlooked the Assiniboine. There

acres to an old French halfbreed named Joseph Plant, near my place. Plant was frozen to death near Pembina, in the winter of 1826, when a lot of the French, who were starving on the plains beyond Pembina, started for the settlement. It was mild at first, but began to rain. The wind changing its direction brought snow and drift, so that they lost the trail. All perished there except a son of Plant, who ran ahead to Grande Pointe, some miles south of Pembina. Though he managed to start a fire, his clothes being wet and he exhausted, he was overcome and died beside the fire, his body being afterwards found near the remains of the small fire. Another son of Plant, who had not been with the party, later on sold the property to John Sutherland, from whom, a few years ago, I purchased it. Old Plant was much liked by the settlers, to whom he was always a very good friend.

Of course I remember Sir George Simpson well. After I married and had a house, he often called upon me, and was very kind and friendly, though, perhaps, I am the only man who ever defied his authority. This took place one time at York Factory when he was walking arm in arm with Sir John Franklin. I wanted a gallon of whisky which had been promised to me, but which he refused to give me. He ordered me to go with the boats for the settlement, which I refused to do until I got my whisky, telling him that I was a colonist and not one of the Company's servants. We were, however, very good friends afterwards. I think the seasons have changed greatly. I can assure you we have had seasons when the strawberries were ripe by June 1. Now they are never ripe before July 1. I think we then had far more birds than now, especially wild fowl and pigeons. I remember when I used to see flocks of pigeons following the course of the river, which were so large that the front of each flock was out of sight in the north, while the tail was out of sight in the south; but they never come now. [In 1871, standing on the spot where now is the junction of Main and Lombard streets, I fired into great flocks of pigeons passing overhead and killed numbers of them.—Ed.]

I have killed Buffalo at Pembina with a knife, having no gun to shoot them. Those were hard days for us.

I commenced freighting to York in 1844.

I was appointed a magistrate in 1852, and acted as such for 18 years, when I retired on account of my deafness.

I remember perfectly the case of the Orkney girl you have written about, who is mentioned, you tell me, in Alexander Henry's journal. Of course I was not in this country in 1807 when the affair occurred, but I knew well the man Scart, who was connected with it, and the story was common talk for many a year after we arrived in the country. I will tell you what I know about it. The girl came out from Orkney to James Bay in the service of the Hudson's Bay Company, and was dressed in man's clothes. For years her sex was not discovered by any of the

people who associated with her. When she was at a post of the company, at James Bay, she was for two years at the Partridge House, with a man named John Scart, who used to find her, on his return from hunting, sitting by the fire crying; and she did very little work, appearing to be much troubled in mind. After that she and Scart were sent inland to Brandon House post, on the Assiniboine River, where they occupied the same cabin in the fort, for in those days a log hut was usually given to each two men. Scart was the right-hand man of Mr. Goodwin, the master at Brandon House for the Hudson's Bay Company, and the latter frequently asked Scart to his house of an evening to take a dram of grog and consult with him. [Henry's unpublished journal contains entry, on 19th of August, 1800, that Robt. Goodwin was in charge of the Hudson's Bay Company's boats for Assiniboine river points. —Ed.]

One night Scart had been at the master's house until late at night, and on his return to the cabin discovered the true sex of his partner. He at once told the frightened woman that he would go to Mr. Goodwin with the news, but she fell on her knees and begged him not to reveal her identity. After much persuasion he consented to keep the secret, and they continued to live together under the same conditions as before, and it was not for a long time after that she lost her honor. She was finally separated from Scart by being sent to Pembina to act as cook for the master there, who went by the name of "Mad McKay." It was when there that she made a discovery as to her condition, and went over to Mr. Henry at the Northwest fort, and was the next morning delivered of a child, to the great surprise of all the people in the country, who had never suspected that she was a woman. [Henry's journal contains a note that on the 15th December, 1807, a young Orkney girl, who had passed as a boy in the H. B. Co.'s service, went to Henry and gave birth to a child. She had followed her lover out from Orkney and he was then at Grand Forks.— Ed.]

The girl was sent back to Orkney with her child. Scart, who always acknowledged the above facts, lived for many years afterwards, dying finally at the Image Plain, below Kildonan. The story was current amongst the early settlers, who knew Scart and Mad McKay, and this was undoubtedly the first white woman who lived in the Red River country. I knew both Baptiste Lajimoniere and his wife, but I never before heard that it was claimed that she was the first white woman in this country. I have often wondered why some person did not write about the Orkney girl, and am glad you are doing so.

GEORGE BANNERMAN, KILDONAN, MAN.

I was born in the Scotland Highlands about 1805, and came to Red River with my parents in 1815.

I remember the time Governor Semple and his people were killed by the French. The bodies were buried near Fort Douglas the day after they were killed. They were buried in one grave near some trees, but I never heard that the remains were taken away from there. I remember Cuthbert Grant, who treated us settlers well, but my memory is not as good as that of Donald Murray, who can give you more information than I can.

The first bricks were made by a man named Hedger, in the flats between Broadway and the fort.

There was a small Indian mound in the vicinity of Seven Oaks, outside the old road.

The first mission buildings erected by the Rev. John West were situated just where the old school house now stands, between the brewery and the college creek.

A person going to Fort Garry would say he was going to the Forks, but thinks it was a general term applied to all the district near the mouth of the Assiniboine.

JOHN MATHESON, OF GRASSMERE, MAN.

The following particulars were obtained from his son, the Rev. Canon Matheson, of St. John's college:

John Matheson was born on October 15, 1814, in the parish of Kildonan, Sutherlandshire, Scotland. He sailed with his parents for York Factory in June, 1815, and arrived at Fort Douglas on Christmas day, of the same year. He was too young to be aware, from personal knowledge, but can speak definitely on the following points:

His deceased brother was present twice at the burying of Governor Semple, the last time being when the bodies were removed from beside Fort Douglas to St. John's churchyard.

Peter Fidler did build a fort nearer the main river than the present one, in the vicinity of Broadway, before 1826, and he knows his father worked for Fidler.

THE LATE ROBERT MACBETH.

Mr. Robert Macbeth was born in Sutherlandshire, Scotland, in 1801. He came out to the Red River with his parents about 1815, as colonists to the Selkirk settlement. He was a successful trader, and for many years a member of the Council of Assiniboine under the Hudson's Bay Company's administration, as well as a magistrate. He was married to Mary Maclean, whom he survived 23 years. He died on the 20th August, 1886, leaving a family of eight to morn his death : Adam, Alexander, Robert, John and Roderick, and Mrs. Angus Henderson, Mrs. John McKay and Mrs. Angustus Mills.

JOHN POLSON, OF KILDONAN, MAN.

I was born in 1810 or thereabouts, in Kildonan, Scotland, and came out with Lord Selkirk's settlers in 1815.

I remember well the seven oak trees which gave the name to the locality, where Governor Semple and his men were killed by the half-breeds, in 1816, and have many

were buried in one large grave, on the afterwards removed to St. John's church-yard. One body, of a man that was killed then, was buried on McDonald's lot, in St. Johns, and the grave was cared for a long while, but is now plowed over and the site lost sight of.

There was an Indian burial mound on the

RED RIVER OX CART.

southwest side of what is now called Logan's crook, and on the property to-day owned by ex-Mayor Logan. There was a clump of trees at the spot when the grave was dug. I do not remember that their bodies were a time shot pheasants (grouse) from their branches.

Governor Semple and some of his people

south side of Seven Oaks creek, near the trail, but it, also, has been plowed over. When people spoke of the Forks, in old times, they referred to the point of land on the north side of the Assiniboine, where that stream flows into the Red. I never heard the south side called the Forks. I have always lived on this lot, and have never been farther away than Portage la Prairie or Pembina since the troubles in 1816.

I remember Fort Gibraltar well, it faced the Red River and the Assiniboine. The rivers were far narrower than they are now. I think I could have thrown a stone across the Red River here then. I remember that bricks were made at St. John's by a man who came out with the Rev. Mr. West.

MRS. KAUFMAN, KILDONAN EAST. MAN.

I was born in Caithness, Scotland, in 1806, and came out here in 1815 with my parents, who were Selkirk colonists. My name was Elizabeth (Betty) McKay before I married Wollrich Kaufman, a DeMeuron soldier, who came up with Lord Selkirk in 1817. Winnipeg was always a great camping ground for the Indians.

I saw Governor Semple and his dead companions buried in one grave on the south side of the creek near Fort Douglas, where a grove of trees stood. The governor and the doctor were buried in coffins, and the others wrapped up in blankets, the day after the massacre. Mr. Sutherland's body was stripped quite naked, but it is not true that they all lay out on the prairie for some days.

I remember that Lord Selkirk came here and held a meeting of the settlers. He was tall and straight, very lordly in appearance, but not strong looking. Before we left Scotland His Lordship promised us a cow each, and a plow between two, but afterwards we had to pay for all these things.

My brother, Selkirk McKay, was born on the way from York Factory, at Painted Stone, being the first white child born in that colony. He was called a fter Lord Selkirk.

I knew Cuthbert Grant very well, for he was very kind to us settlers.

I remember the stockade fort Donald Murray speaks of. It was between Fort Douglas and the Northwest fort. I cannot now tell you where it was, for the ground is all covered with houses, but I think it was near the high ground between the forts. This fort was existing at the same time as the colony fort and the Northwest Company's place.

Go to Donald Murray, he can tell you far more than any of us about these things.

[Father Dugast, of St. Boniface, has written most interesting notes of the history of Mme. Lajimoniere, a French-Canadian woman who arrived at Pembina, from Montreal, in 1806, and it has been stated by several writers that she was the first white woman in the Red River country. The above evidence proves these statements to be not founded on fact, and though they have been made in good faith, it is well they should be denied.—ED.]

THE LAST OF FORT GARRY.